HORSE
and
PONY
DICTIONARY

HORSE
and
PONY
DICTIONARY

Robert Owen

COUNTRY LIFE
BOOKS

Other books by the author include:

My Learn to Ride Book (1971)
Successful Riding and Jumping (1975)
Horses and Ponies (1978)
The Country Life Book of the Horse (1979)
Riding and Jumping (1983)

Published by Country Life Books,
an imprint of Newnes Books,
a Division of The Hamlyn Publishing Group Limited
84–88 The Centre, Feltham, Middlesex, England
and distributed for them by
The Hamlyn Publishing Group Limited
Rushden, Northants, England.

First published 1981 as *The Beaver Horse and Pony Dictionary*
This edition first published 1984

ISBN 0 600 35707 4

Phototypeset by Input Typesetting Ltd, London

Printed in England

Preface

This dictionary, first published as a paperback, has been revised. It was compiled to list and define some of the many words and phrases used when discussing or describing the world of horses and ponies. It is also intended to be of interest to readers wishing to identify the technical and colloquial terms used in the specialist journals and in the many books dealing with equestrian activities to be found in libraries and bookshops.

To bring together in one volume the many thousands of words which relate to the world of horses would be an impossible task, as the subject would demand several books of this size. I have been extremely selective, and I am aware of much that has been omitted.

Among the words in this dictionary are some of foreign origin which are now in general use – words such as *dressage, chef d'équipe, cavalletti* and *pirouette*. I have also introduced the names of some well-known horses, riding personalities and locations.

The subject matter is huge, and I hope that this compilation will help younger people to enjoy a wider appreciation and understanding of their interest by learning about the words and phrases which are such an integral part of the world of horses and ponies.

R.O.

A

ABRS Association of British Riding Schools.

AHSA American Horse Shows Association.

AIT Area International Trial. A show-jumping competition held in the areas administered by the British Show Jumping Association (BSJA). The winners of each competition qualify to compete at the Royal International Horse Show held each July: men, for the King George V Gold Cup; women for the Queen Elizabeth II Cup.

acacia a tree or shrub to be found in fields and hedgerows. Can be highly dangerous to horses and ponies when eaten in excess.

acorns the fruit of the oak tree. Can be highly dangerous when eaten in large quantities. Fallen acorns should be collected and destroyed.

action the movement of a horse or pony in the various paces or gaits.

adjustable head collar a type of head collar with an adjustable headstrap, noseband and throat strap.

affiliated show a horse show which is affiliated to one or more of the recognised societies or associations governing different aspects of equestrian sport, and at which the rules of the society or association apply.

against the clock a term used in show-jumping where, in the event of two or more competitors being equal at the end of a first or second round, they jump a final round where time may also play a part in determining the placings. Unless there has been an outright winner, either by having jumped a clear round, or with fewer faults than any other competitor, the winner is found in a final round by the lowest number of faults and the fastest time. (See also *Tables*.)

aged   a horse aged seven years or more.

ageing   the method by which the age of a horse or pony is established. (See illustration opposite.)

aids   **1** the signals given by a rider to convey instructions to a horse or pony; **2** the means by which the signals are produced. The two types of aids are: the *natural* aids, produced by the use of a rider's body weight, legs, hands and voice; and the *artificial* aids, by the use of whips, spurs and martingales.

Alken, Henry Thomas   the younger brother of Samuel Alken, and father of Samuel Henry Alken, all members of a family of sporting artists. Henry Thomas Alken was famous for his paintings of equestrian scenes, and for the many books he illustrated. Born 1795; died 1851.

all-purpose saddle   see *saddle, general-purpose*.

amble   a slow walk or trot used extensively in the show rings in the United States of America.

American quarter horse   a breed developed by the early settlers in the United States. Standing up to 15 hands, the quarter horse is found in many countries of the world. From the latter part of the seventeenth century, this breed, with its great speed over short distances, has been used particularly as a racehorse over straight quarter-mile races.

American Horse Shows Association   see *AHSA*.

American Standardbred   a powerfully built horse used in trotting and harness racing. Height between 15 and 16 hands; colours: bay, black, brown and chestnut.

anaemia   a condition which demands treatment by a veterinary surgeon. Anaemia arises from a lack of haemoglobin in the blood, the most immediate sign being a lack of strength and stamina, and more rapid breathing than normal after exertion.

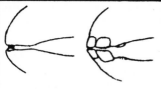

Birth to 6 months: The temporary incisors or milk teeth begin to appear after 10 days.

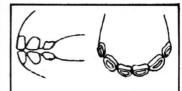

2 years: There is now a full set of milk teeth, showing small dark rings on the biting edges.

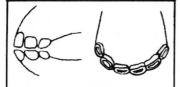

3 years: First permanent teeth. At first they show no marks, but these soon appear.

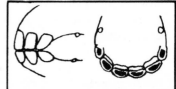

5 years: A 'full mouth' of permanent teeth. Corner incisors meet only at the front.

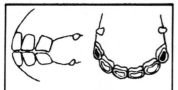

7 years: Corner incisors now meet, and a small hook appears on the upper corner incisors.

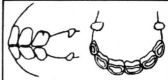

9 years: 'Galvayne's Groove' appears at top corner incisors. At this age it is about 3 mm (1/8 inch) long.

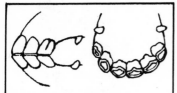

15 years: Teeth have become more triangular and are beginning to slope out.

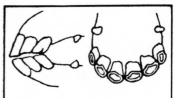

25 years: Slope of incisors is very pronounced. 'Galvayne's Groove' is disappearing.

Andalucian   a breed from Andalucia in Spain. After the Arab and Thoroughbred, the Andalucian has had great influence on the horse we know today. Its ancestry goes back many centuries, long before the Spanish explorers of the fifteenth and sixteenth centuries were opening up the New World. The pure-bred Andalucian makes an excellent riding horse, though has never been established outside Spain as a major breed.

Anglo-Arab   in England the Arab Horse Society recognises the Anglo-Arab as a cross from a Thoroughbred stallion and an Arab mare or from an Arab stallion and a Thoroughbred mare. In other parts of the world the percentage of Arabian blood varies in the Anglo-Arabs found. The Anglo-Arab has outstanding qualities, with the best of the Thoroughbred and the carriage and grace of the Arab. It is used increasingly as a hunter, hack and showjumper, and as a ridden horse in other equestrian activities.

ankle boots   the protective covering worn around the fetlocks of a horse or pony. See also *brushing boots*.

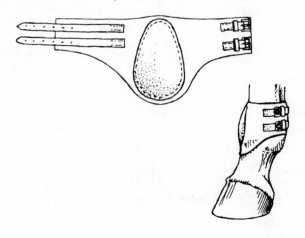

Anne, HRH The Princess, Mrs Mark Phillips (Great Britain) won the individual European Championship at Burghley in 1971, and a silver medal for the individual European Championship in 1975. She rode for Great Britain in the 1976 Three-day Event at the Olympic Games.

anodynes medicine or drugs which relieve or remove pain.

Ansell, Colonel Sir Michael (Great Britain) a leading personality in the world of show jumping. It is largely through his efforts that show jumping has become the major international sport it is today.

anti-cast roller a stable roller specially designed with a metal hoop or arch to prevent a horse from becoming cast after rolling. (See page 29.) Known also as an *arch roller*.

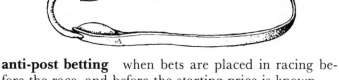

anti-post betting when bets are placed in racing before the race, and before the starting price is known.

anti-sweat sheet an open-mesh cotton sheet or rug used after a horse or pony has been at exercise or work. The mesh creates small pockets of air next to the horse's skin, thus preventing the body temperature from falling too rapidly.

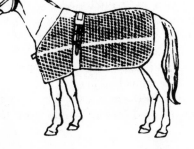

anvil   an iron base used by a farrier on which horse-shoes are shaped.

Appaloosa   a spotted horse from the Palouse district of Idaho in the United States, though now found in many countries throughout the world. The Appaloosa is mostly grey with dark round or oval spots on the back and quarters.

apprentice   a young person being trained as a jockey. Apprenticeships extend for a period of between five and seven years.

apron   **1** a farrier's apron is made from hide with a pocket or type of pouch. It is split in the centre to enable the farrier to handle a horse's leg more easily; **2** in driving, the apron is a rug worn across the knees of the driver to keep the wearer clean, dry and warm. The material used in the making of an apron varies from a light form of linen through to much heavier waterproofed and lined cloths.

Arab   the breed which has been most influential in the development of the horse we know today. Originally from Arabia and desert areas, the Arab is now widely bred throughout the world, particularly in the United States and Great Britain. It is the oldest of all known breeds. The founder sires of the Thoroughbred were three Arabians – Byerley Turk, Godolphin Arabian and Darley Arabian – who were brought to Great Britain during the early years of the seventeenth century.

   The Arab has many characteristics which distinguish it from other breeds. It has a head of great beauty and alertness with a 'dished' face, a tail which is carried higher than that of most other horses, and an overall appearance of strength and grace. Arabs are renowned for their intelligence and stamina. Most stand between 14 and 15 hands and are found in bay, grey and chestnut, with an occasional black.

arch-mouth Pelham   a bit having a mouthpiece with a distinct upward curve, giving more tongue room.

arch roller   see *anti-cast roller*.

Ardennais   a breed of heavy horse from the Ardennes and widely used in France as a draught horse. Standing up to 16 hands, the Ardennais is strong, thick-set and muscular. The breed, also known as Ardennes, is also extensively used in its place of origin – the south-east corner of Belgium.

artificial aids   see *aids*.

artificial pace   a pace or gait taught to many horses in the United States – the amble or the rack (see pages 8 and 97). An artificial pace is additional to the normal walk, trot, canter and gallop.

artzel   a white mark on the forehead.

Ascot   a racecourse close to Windsor Castle and owned by HM The Queen. It is administered by a non-profit-making organisation known as the Ascot Authority. Racing first took place there during the reign of Queen Anne. The main meeting, 'Royal Ascot' is held each June, and before racing begins each day a colourful procession of open carriages takes place, bringing members of the Royal Family and their guests from Windsor Castle.

Asiatic Wild Horse   one of the remaining breeds which have descended from 'primitive' horses. They were established many thousands of years ago, and those seen today, mostly in zoos, have altered little during the intervening years. The breed was discovered in Mongolia by Colonel Przrewalskii in 1881. The Asiatic Wild Horse is also known as a Steppe Horse or *Equus Przrewalskii Przrewalskii Poliakov*.

'asking the question'   an expression used when a horse or pony has been ridden to the limit, or is asked to make an extra effort.

ass   a slow, patient, sure-footed beast of burden found in many countries. The domesticated ass is a descendant of the wild ass, the male being known as a jackass, and the female as a she-ass.

Atherstone girth   a girth made from baghide (cow hide) and shaped to allow extra movement at a horse's elbow, preventing chafing and galling.

auction   a public sale at which horses and ponies are sold to the highest bidder.

Australian Simplex Safety iron   a type of stirrup with a strap device at one side to allow easy release of a rider's foot.

automatic timing   a device using an electric beam which is broken once a horse or pony crosses a start or a finish line.

azoturia   a disease of horses which may occur at any time during the year. The cause of azoturia is not easy to determine, but it is sometimes felt to be associated with feeding. One of the noticeable effects of the disease is a hardening of the muscles of the loins and quarters. If azoturia is suspected a veterinary surgeon should be called.

B

BDS British Driving Society.
BEF British Equestrian Federation.
BHS British Horse Society.
BHSAI British Horse Society Assistant Instructor.
BHSI British Horse Society Instructor.
BSJA British Show Jumping Association.
BSPS British Show Pony Society.
backing mounting a young horse or pony as part of its breaking-in.
Badminton Horse Trials the world's major three-day event which takes place at Badminton House, the home of the Duke of Beaufort, in Gloucestershire. The three phases of the event are: dressage; the speed, endurance and cross-country test over a combined course of approximately 26 kilometres (16 miles); and show jumping. The winner receives the coveted Whitbread Cup.
balance a word to describe the state of a horse or pony which has its own weight, plus the weight of a rider, spread evenly over each leg to enable it to use itself with the maximum ease and efficiency. A horse running 'free' is able at all times to adjust its own balance, but its balance can quickly be upset once a rider is being carried. Good, correct balance is achieved through exercise and schooling, supported by a rider's awareness, skill and experience.
balance strap a strap forming part of a side-saddle.
bald face the white marking seen on the head of a

horse or pony extending to cover the muzzle and part of the jaw.

Balding girth a plaited type of girth, designed, as the Atherstone, to prevent chafing and galling.

Ball, Alan the senior course designer for the BSJA.

Ballsbridge the permanent showground in Dublin, setting for the Dublin Horse Sales and the Dublin International Horse Show.

bandages the three types of bandages most commonly in use are: the tail bandage, used for protection and to keep the hairs in place; the stable bandage, used for warmth or protection of the legs in the stable or when travelling, and the exercise bandage, used on the legs when at work. Bandages, which are made from cotton, wool, crêpe, stockinette, flannel or nylon, should never be tightly fitted and are frequently applied over a padding of gamgee or other tissue.

bank **1** a built-up mound used in some show jumping competitions. Perhaps the best-known of all being the Hickstead bank used in the show-jumping 'Derby'; **2** a horse or pony is said to 'bank' when jumping the middle part of an oxer or spread obstacle and, believing it to be solid, attempts to jump off.

Barb a breed of horse originally from North Africa, particularly from the area known as Barbary – Morocco, Algeria and Tunisia. It has qualities similar to the Arab, being both speedy and having great endurance. Very few true Barbs are to be found today. They stand between 14 and 15 hands, and the predominant colours are brown, bay, chestnut, grey and black.

barbed wire   the use of barbed wire is never advised to fence in any field or paddock. All animals tend to rub up against fencing and trees, and if they do this against barbed wire it can cause skin wounds and lacerations. Regular checks must be carried out to ensure all fencing is secure and, in the case of wire, to see this is not broken or in a dangerous condition.

barley   a cereal which may be used occasionally as an alternative to oats, or as a supplement to normal feeding. Barley is best when crushed and boiled.

barley straw   a material used for bedding.

barouche   an open four-wheeled carriage used during the early part of the nineteenth century. A barouche has always been considered an elegant means of travel, and is driven either from the high box seat or from a ridden postillion. Two barouches, which are used for official occasions, are to be found in the Royal Mews in London.

barrage   a word used in place of 'jump-off'.

barrel   the part of the body of a horse which extends from behind the forearms to the loins.

bars of the mouth   the space on the lower jaw, between the canine teeth (tushes) and the molars, on which a bit rests. (See illustration on page 9.)

bars of a saddle   the metal fittings under the skirt of a saddle to which the leathers are attached.

bay (colour)   a brown body with black mane and tail, and perhaps some black marks on the limbs.

bedding   the materials used to make a bed – wheat straw, barley straw, wood shavings, wood chips, sawdust or bracken.

bed down   to prepare and make a bed.

Bedford cart   a two-wheeled cart used by farmers and dealers. The seating arrangement is similar to that found in a dog cart, with two people facing forwards and two backwards.

behind the bit   an expression used where a horse or pony refuses to take hold of the bit and does everything possible to evade it. Contact with the bit is essential, and any animal which is 'behind the bit' must be taught to take hold and not resist.

Belgian Ardennes the earliest of the Belgian heavy breeds. The Ardennes, or Ardennais, is compact and strong, with a wide and deep chest and massive short legs, making it ideally suited to work in hilly country. Colours: bay, chestnut, roan. Stands between 14.2 and 15.3 hands.

bent-top iron a stirrup iron which is made with the top part curved away from the rider's instep.

bib martingale a form of running martingale with a triangular-shaped centrepiece. See illustration page 78.

bit a bar-like device made from rubber, vulcanite or metal and attached to both the bridle and reins. It is the means by which pace and direction are controlled. The bit also regulates the position of the horse's head carriage. There are a number of different bits in use today, and these generally are grouped under four headings: the snaffle, the Weymouth, the Pelham, and the gag. See illustration opposite.

bitless bridle a bitless bridle acts on the chin groove and nose rather than on the bars of the mouth. The best-known bitless bridle in use today is the Hackamore. This consists of two metal cheek-pieces curved round the nose by means of leather attachments. Any bitless bridle

Bitless bridle

can be most severe and is not advised for use by younger riders. As from 1st January 1984 the BSJA have introduced a new rule which states that Hackamores and bitless bridles are not permitted in pony competitions.

black (colour) a black horse or pony is one with a black body and black mane and tail. Most so-called

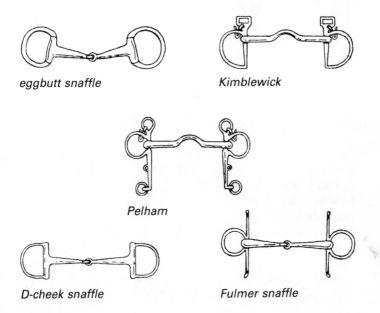

eggbutt snaffle

Kimblewick

Pelham

D-cheek snaffle

Fulmer snaffle

black horses can, on close inspection, be found to have some white showing through. In all countries other than the United States, a horse with some white markings on the face and limbs is accepted as black.

Black Beauty   a classic story by Anna Sewell, first published in 1877.

Black Bess   the mare ridden by Dick Turpin on his legendary ride from London to York.

black points   the black mane, tail and lower parts of the legs found on bay and brown horses.

blacksmith   see *farrier*.

Blair bridle   a type of bitless bridle with extra long cheek-pieces.

blankets   a form of protective clothing, including day rugs, night rugs, summer sheets, anti-sweat sheets, New Zealand rugs, etc.

blanket clip   the name given to the clip when the hair is taken from the neck and belly, leaving a blanket-shaped patch over the back, top of the flanks and the quarters. See illustration on page 33.

blaze   a broad white mark running down the face.

blemish   a scar which remains after an injury or wound has healed, which in no way affects a horse or pony's performance or health.

blinkers   the wearing of blinkers, other than in horse-racing and driving, is not permitted in any equestrian activity or sport.

blood   the amount of blood in a horse's body is approximately one-eighteenth of its body weight.

blood-horse   a Thoroughbred.

bloom   the shine of the coat.

blue dun   see *dun*.

bobtailed   a horse with a short, docked tail.

body brush   an oval-shaped brush set with fine bristles. It has a strap across the back through which the hand is placed. A body brush is used to clean dust, scurf and loose hairs from the horse's body. It also helps to stimulate the horse's circulation. After each stroke, the brush should be drawn across the teeth of a curry comb to remove the dirt. (See illustration on page 56.)

bog spavin   a non-painful swelling of the bone on the inner and front part of the hock joint.

bolting   a word indicating 'out of control'.

bone   the 'bone' of a horse is measured just below the knee, a measurement which tells much to an experienced horseman or veterinary surgeon.

bone spavin   a hard bony swelling on the inside lower edge of the hock joint. It is a condition brought about by strain or injury, and is acutely painful.

bootjack   a device made from metal or wood designed to help the removal of riding boots.

boring   a horse or pony leaning heavily on the bit is said to be 'boring'.

boss   an ornamental circular decoration fitted to a bridle.

botfly   see *gadfly*.

Boulonnais   a breed of heavy horse from the Boulogne district in north-western France. A big-standing, strong draught horse, the Boulonnais is used by farmers. The breed has had a great influence on other draught horses coming from France and Belgium.

box   **1** the seat on a coach or carriage used by the driver or coachman; **2** the conveyance used to transport a horse or pony, or the action of transporting him; **3** a stable, see *loose box*.

boxy feet   having a 'donkey' foot with a high heel and an upright appearance, as shown in the illustration.

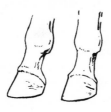

bracken an alternative bedding material.

Bradley, Caroline (Great Britain) who died shortly after completing a round in a show-jumping competition during 1983. She was one of the world's leading lady show jumpers having regularly represented Great Britain in international competitions. Caroline was a hard-working and dedicated rider who won an enormous number of competitions throughout the British Isles, especially on the brilliant stallion Marius and the handsome grey Hanoverian, Tigre.

bradoon see *bridoon*.

braiding a word used in the United States for plaiting.

brake a widely used four-wheeled vehicle which came into popular use during the middle part of the nineteenth century.

bran a foodstuff made from ground or milled wheat. It adds bulk to a feed, is good for digestion, and forms a basis for a bran or linseed mash. Care must be taken not to overfeed bran, and advice on quantity should be obtained from a veterinary surgeon or from a horseman who has wide experience in the care and keeping of horses and ponies.

bran mash to make a bran mash; mix, say, 1.8 kg (4 lb) of bran with boiling water. Add a pinch of salt. Stir together into a smooth (not running) mixture, then place a sack or towel over the bucket and leave to cool before feeding.

break **1** to train or school a young horse or pony; **2** to change pace (gait), e.g. to move from a walk into a trot a rider will be said to 'break' into the trot.

breaking the training of a young horse. See *break* above.

breaking-out a sign of sudden sweating, usually associated with excitement.

breastplate the piece of equipment, made from leather, which is attached to a saddle and goes round the horse's breast to prevent the saddle from slipping back. Known also as a breastpiece.

Breton a light draught horse, bred in the Brittany region of France, and standing between 15 and 16.1 hands. Colours: mostly red roan, chestnut, bay and grey.

bridle the several different types of bridle can be placed in one of five groups: the snaffle; the Weymouth; the Pelham; the gag; the bitless bridle. Various parts of the bridle, common to all groups, include the headpiece; the cheek-pieces, to which the bit is fitted; the throat latch or throat lash; the browband; the noseband, and the reins. The illustration on page 24 shows the component parts for the Weymouth or double bridle.

bridle, behind the a horse or pony not being well up to the bit may be said to be 'behind the bridle'.

bridle, in front of the the opposite of being behind the bridle; when a horse or pony is tending to take too much hold.

bridle, parts of (See illustration on page 24.)

bridoon the snaffle bit used in a Weymouth or double bridle. There are many types of bridoon – plain, twisted, eggbutt, etc. Sometimes known as a *bradoon*.

Brinckmann, Hans (West Germany) once a most successful international rider, now placed among the world's leading course designers and builders.

British native ponies the nine recognised breeds are: Connemara, Dales, Dartmoor, Exmoor, Fell, Highland, New Forest, Shetland and Welsh.

broken wind is a term which covers various chronic lung conditions. Where broken wind is caused by an allergy, it is possible to relieve the effects by removing all sources of dust in the stable, feeding only good quality hay which must be given when damp, and avoiding bulk foods. Linseed oil, fed about three times a week, will also help. Since dust is always apparent in straw it is advisable to change to wood shavings. One of the symptoms of broken wind is a deep and long-drawn-out cough.

brood mare a mare used for breeding.

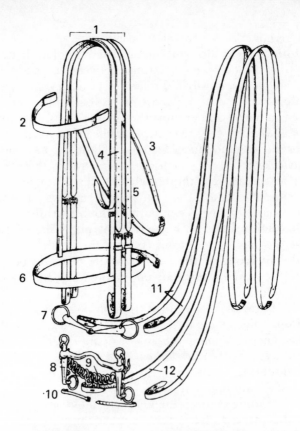

Parts of a double bridle; 1 headpiece; 2 browband; 3 throatlash; 4 cheek-piece for Weymouth bit; 5 cheek-piece for bridoon bit; 6 noseband; 7 bridoon (snaffle) bit; 8 Weymouth (curb) bit; 9 curb chain; 10 lipstrap; 11 snaffle reins; 12 curb reins

Broome, David (Great Britain) among the world's leading show jumpers. Born in Cardiff, he has had immense success in his chosen sport, winning the Men's World Championship in 1970; the European Championship in 1961, 1967 and 1969, and Olympic bronze medals in 1960 and 1968, and was a member of the gold medal team in the World Championships in 1978.

browband the part of the bridle which lies across the horse's forehead. Usually made from a plain leather strap, browbands are also found in various colours. Another word for browband is *front*.

brown a colour with a mixture of brown and black though not to be confused with the bay colour. Most brown horses have dark-brown manes and tails, though some, like the bay, have black points.

Brumby a wild horse found in Australia. Most of these are claimed to be descended from the saddle horses which have strayed from cattle stations.

brush the tail of a fox.

brushing the act caused by a horse or pony's leg striking the opposite leg on the inner part of the fetlock. The most common form of brushing is when a hindleg comes into contact with a foreleg.

brushing boots protective boots made from leather with a padded section running down the inside to give protection against brushing.

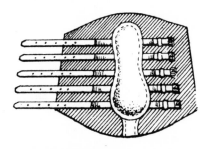

bucking the act of leaping into the air, often with the intention of trying to dislodge or unseat the rider.

buffer one of the tools used by a farrier.

Burghley Horse Trials a major three-day event held in September each year at Burghley House in Lincolnshire.

burro a donkey.

bute see *phenylbutazone*.

buttermilk horse   the name given to a Palomino in the western regions of the United States of America.

Byerley Turk   one of the three founding sires of the English Thoroughbred. Brought to England in 1689 by Captain Robert Byerley. See also *Darley Arabian* and *Godolphin Arabian*.

C

caballo the Spanish word for horse.

cabriolet a high, single-horse, two-wheeled vehicle used throughout most of the nineteenth century as a form of taxi. The word 'cab', which is still in use, is a shortened form of the word cabriolet.

cade a foal raised by hand.

cadence a term used in dressage for the rhythm and tempo of a pace, during which a horse attempts to cover an equal space of ground in an equal space of time.

Cadre Noir the group of black-uniformed instructors who teach riding in the French classical tradition. They are based at the cavalry school at Saumur, France, which in recent times has become attached to the École Nationale d'Équitation (the National School of Equitation).

Camargue a breed from the delta area of the River Rhône in France, almost always grey in colour. The paintings found on the walls of caves at Niaux and Lascaux resemble closely the early Camargue horse. These paintings are dated about 1500 BC.

camp a horse standing with its forelegs and hind legs spread as wide as possible is said to be standing 'camp'. Also known as 'stretching'.

cannon bone the bone of a foreleg which extends between the knee and fetlock. The corresponding bone in a hind leg is known as a shank.

canter one of the natural paces (gaits), a canter is made up in three-time. When cantering to the right this sequence should be near hind, near fore and off hind together (known as a left diagonal) and off fore (the leading leg). It is said the word 'canter' came from a type of gallop used by the pilgrims when on their way to Canterbury.

canter, collected a slow collected pace (gait) with good impulsion and very active quarters.

canters, extended a pace of the canter when the stride is longer than in the normal canter.

canter, false a canter is false when a horse or pony, moving on a curved track, is leading with the wrong leg. When a 'false' canter is deliberately used it is known as a counter canter.

canter, true a true canter is seen when a horse, moving on a curved track, has the correct leg leading. For example, when turning on a left-hand track the near side foreleg would be leading.

cantle the back of the saddle.

capped hock a swelling on the joint of the hock which might be caused by one of several reasons: kicking, damage from a stable floor if there is a shortage of bedding, an injury when travelling, etc.

capriole a movement in *haute école* (high school). The horse, with its hocks drawn under its body, rears and jumps into the air, kicking out the hind legs and finally landing square on all four legs. The horses at the Spanish Riding School in Vienna are renowned for their display which includes the capriole.

carousel a musical ride.

carrots vegetables enjoyed by most horses and ponies. They should be fed cut into lengths rather than fed whole or in chunks.

cart some of the different parts of Great Britain had their own 'local' cart. These included the Norfolk cart, the Essex cart and the Yorkshire cart. Other carts were named after the coach-builder – the Morgan cart and the Craven cart are two. Some were named after the purpose for which they were built, e.g. dog cart, donkey cart, luggage cart, governess cart, etc.

carted a term used for a rider whose horse or pony has run away.

cast **1** a horse or pony, when lying down in a box or against a wall and unable to get up, is cast; **2** when a horse or pony has lost a shoe.

cavalletti trestle-type jumps which are adjustable in height though the cross-bar is fixed. Widely used in schooling and as practice obstacles.

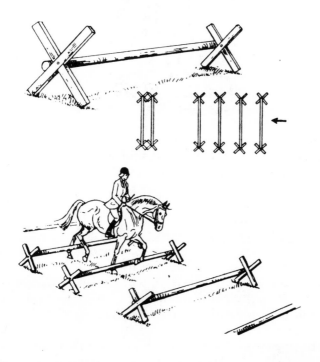

cavesson there are two types of cavesson nosebands. One, the plain cavesson; two, the lungeing cavesson. The latter is a specially designed head collar which has a padded nose-piece. To this is fixed a metal plate and three metal swivelling rings. The lunge rein is attached to either of the rings. See illustration page 83.

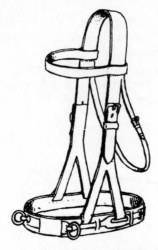

Lungeing cavesson

chaff chopped hay or straw which adds bulk to feeds.
chaise a low, two-wheeled vehicle widely used by ladies during the nineteenth century. The word *chaise* is the French word for 'chair'.
champ a horse or pony is said to champ when it chews and mouths its bit.
change of leg a movement at the canter in which the horse is brought back to the walk or trot and re-started with the opposite or other leg leading. For example, at a canter with left (near) foreleg leading, the pace is reduced and a positive change is made to enable the right (off) fore to become the leading leg. See also *flying change*.
cheek-piece **1** a part of a bridle (see illustration page 24); **2** the side of a curb or Pelham bit; **3** the part of a snaffle bit which forms a straight bar, as seen on a Fulmer. (See illustrations on page 19.)
chef d'équipe the person who manages and some-

times captains an equestrian team, especially at international competitions.

chesnut the traditional Suffolk spelling for any of the seven shades of colour of the Suffolk Punch heavy horses.

chestnut 1 a colour which is basically a reddish-brown, often with a lighter mane and tail. Three different colours of chestnut are found; light chestnut, liver chestnut and dark chestnut; 2 a small growth found on the inside of a leg, above the knee and below the hock; known also as a castor.

cheval the French word for a horse.

chukka a period of play in a game of polo. The full game is eight chukkas, but under Hurlingham Polo Association Rules six chukkas are played. Each chukka is timed to last for seven minutes, after which time a bell is rung. The game goes on until the ball goes out of play, or for another 30 seconds, when the bell is rung again and the teams leave the field, the chukka ending wherever the ball happens to be. In the case of a tie at the end of the game an additional chukka is played, and the first team scoring is declared the winner. There are intervals of three minutes between each chukka and five minutes at half time.

cinch a type of leather girth used in the United States. A cinch has rings, not buckles, on each end which are threaded through straps to fasten them to the saddle.

cinch up, to an expression used in the United States to describe fastening a girth.

circle a circle in jumping which causes a competitor to cross his track before jumping the next obstacle, a refusal, run-out or other disobedience is penalised. Once a disobedience has taken place and recorded by the judges, a competitor may turn a circle without any further penalty in the process of his returning to the correct track.

clean bred a pure-bred.

clean leg a leg without blemishes or signs of injury.

clean-legged legs with little hair round the fetlocks such as those of riding horses and ponies, and of heavy horses like the Suffolk Punch as opposed to those of the Shire or Clydesdale. See *feather*.

clean round see *clear round*.

clear round a term used in show-jumping and other equestrian activities indicating that a competitor has completed a course without penalties of any kind.

cleft a part of the frog of the horse's foot. See pages 52–3.

clench the pointed end of a nail used to fix a shoe. Clenches are 'cut off' or 'wrung off' and hammered down flat against the wall of the hoof. One regular part of stable routine, and this includes checking those animals kept at grass, is to see that clenches (sometimes called clinches) have not 'risen', leaving sharp and dangerous points.

Cleveland Bay a breed of horse from the north-eastern part of Yorkshire. Popular with those who drive, the Cleveland Bay stands up to 16 hands. As the name implies, the breed must be bay-coloured, though a small star is permitted.

clinch see *clench*.

clipping the act of removing hair from the body of horses and ponies. Clipping-out becomes essential for horses and ponies in work during autumn and winter months, when the coats grow thicker. Horses and ponies will quickly lose condition should they sweat-up after being ridden hard, and clipping is an all-important act towards the animals' welfare.

clips, types of 1 the *trace clip*, which removes the hair from the under-body and along the front of the neck. With this clip no hair is taken from the legs, back or quarters; 2 the *blanket clip*, similar to the trace clip, in that the hair is removed from the under-side of the body, but in addition the hair from the neck and head is removed and cut square to where a blanket would reach when covering the withers and shoulders; **3** the *hunter clip* which removes all hair, with the exception of the legs and a small patch where a saddle would rest; **4** the *full clip*, which removes hair from all parts.

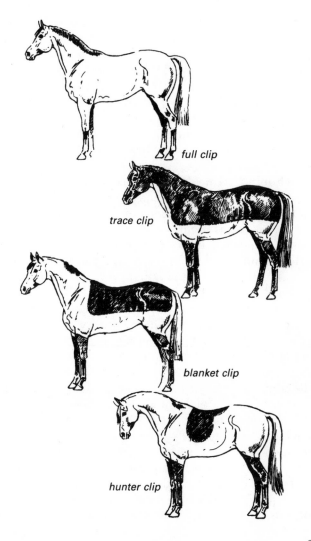

full clip

trace clip

blanket clip

hunter clip

clothing a word embracing the miscellaneous equipment for a horse or pony including that which comes under the heading of saddlery or tack.

club feet a term describing small, boxy-type feet. (See page 21.)

Clydesdale a heavy horse from Scotland, used in agriculture and for pulling drays in city streets. Clydesdales are also popular at agricultural displays and horse shows throughout the country. They stand between 16.2 and 17 hands, and are mostly bay, brown, grey and black.

cob a type of horse, not a breed; strong and short-legged. See *hack, hunter, polo pony.*

cock horse an additional horse which was added to the front of a team to help when pulling heavy loads up hills.

cold shoeing a method of shoeing, now widely used, where the shoes or plates are previously made-up and shaped and not forged specifically to fit the animal being shod. Some adjustments to ensure fit can be made to shoes used in the cold-shoeing method.

colic an illness of the digestive system. Colic is sometimes due to a too sudden change of diet or by giving poor quality feed. The first signs will be an indication that the horse or pony is in pain. He will most probably want to lie down and roll. The veterinary surgeon should be called if the symptoms continue for more than forty-five minutes, but the best immediate treatment is to walk the sick animal.

collected a horse or pony is collected when being ridden well up to the bit with good impulsion. The animal must have maximum control over its limbs and movements and be completely responsive to the rider's aids.

collected trot a trot with shorter steps than used in a normal trot, but a pace (gait) having plenty of impulsion which must be controlled by the rider. All 'collected' paces (gaits) are rhythmic and quietly controlled.

collecting ring the area adjacent to the showing or

show-jumping ring where horses or ponies are collected prior to entering a competition and coming in front of the judges.

colours 1 the name given to the 'silks' worn by jockeys; **2** the principal body colours of the equine. These are also known as the solid colours, and are: bay, brown, black, chestnut, grey, dun and roan. Piebald and skewbald are also recognised colours, though are not 'solid'. Where doubt exists, and all horses and ponies slightly change colour during the different seasons or as they become older, reference is made to the colours of the points – the muzzle, tips of the ears, mane and tail. White is not a recognised colour, it is a lighter shade of grey.

colt a young ungelded male horse up to four years of age.

combination in show jumping a combination may be made up from two or three separate elements (fences) each of which can be of a different design, though the two or three elements together count as one single obstacle. Any refusal, run-out, fall or knock down at any element in a combination is penalised as for a single obstacle. Refusals and other disobediences mean the entire combination having to be jumped before moving on to another obstacle. Elements knocked down during the act of jumping a combination each count as four faults. All penalties incurred are added together to give one total for the combination. A fall between elements of a combination is treated as for a fall anywhere else on the course, and counts as eight faults.

combined system the combined system of keeping a horse or pony is where the animal is put out to graze by day and brought into the stable at night. In very hot weather this can be reversed, and the horse or pony is kept in during the day and allowed to graze at night.

combined training the name given to embrace one-, two-, or three-day events. Today, these are grouped under a generic heading of Horse Trials.

combs   plastic or metal combs with widely spaced teeth which can be used for a mane or tail. See also *curry comb*.

condition   a term used to describe the health and appearance of a horse or pony.

conformation   a word meaning 'shape' or the way a horse or pony is 'put together'. The study and understanding of all that contributes to good or bad conformation is most complex and is acquired by some people after a lifetime spent with horses. Conformation plays a critical part when horses are being bought or judged (other than in show-jumping competitions) when overall appearance, plus the set and lie of some of the points of the horse are taken into account.

Connemara   one of the nine British native pony breeds. The Connemara comes from the western part of Ireland. Mostly grey, dun, dark brown and chestnut, they are versatile, hardy and likeable riding ponies, standing between 13 and 14.2 hands.

contact   the 'feel' or link through the reins between the hands of the rider and the mouth of the horse or pony. Contact must always be light, and some form of contact, even that of the weight of the reins alone, should be maintained at all times when riding.

Copenhagen   the horse ridden by the Duke of Wellington at the Battle of Waterloo in 1815.

corns   these are likely to form on the sole of a foot in the heel region when shoes have been badly fitted.

coronary band   a sensitive part of a horse or pony's foot which lies in the coronary groove around the upper edge of the wall.

coronet   a coronary band found at the top of the hoof.

cough   any cough in a horse or pony is a sign of unsoundness and, at the first indication, an animal must be taken out of work. Various types of coughs are to be found, and diagnosis and treatment is essential. Can be contagious and a veterinary surgeon must be called.

counter lead   the name given to cantering on the right rein with the near foreleg leading, or cantering on the left rein with the off foreleg leading.

country   a term used in hunting to describe the territory hunted.

couple   in hunting the word is used to denote two hounds. Hounds are always counted in this manner. Most packs hunt with an odd number of hounds, e.g. fifteen and a half couple, meaning thirty-one hounds.

course   a sequence of obstacles found in show jumping or when riding in a cross-country competition.

course plan   the plan, showing the sequence of obstacles to be jumped. Before the start of a competition this is handed to the judges and also displayed in the collecting ring. A course plan shows the time allowed and time limit for the course, together with the speed of jumping. It also indicates the fences or obstacles to be jumped in any jump-off.

covert   (pronounced cover) a term used in hunting for a small wood or copse.

cow hocks   hocks which turn inwards at the points.

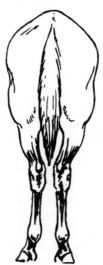

Cow hocks

cracked heels an inflammation of the skin found in the hollow of the heel.

cracks these may appear in the wall of the foot and are given specific names referring to the position, e.g. toe-cracks, side-cracks, bar-cracks, etc. Sandcracks appear over the entire wall.

cradle a wooden collar device fitted round the neck of a horse or pony to prevent him from licking or biting an affected area or treated injury.

crash helmet specially designed skull caps which must be worn under the rules of racing, and which are becoming increasingly popular with those riding cross-country or at hunter trials.

Craven cart a two-wheeled vehicle introduced at the turn of the century. The driver and one passenger sat on a forward-facing seat; two additional passengers were seated behind facing backwards.

cream (colour) a cream-coloured coat with unpigmented skin and usually found with a flaxen mane and tail.

crest the ridge running along the back of a horse or pony's neck and the part from which the mane grows.

crib a manger.

crib biting a harmful vice mostly caused by boredom in which the crib or door is gripped and chewed with the incisor teeth.

crop whip.

cross-breeding when pure-bred horses and ponies of different breeds are mated.

cross-country a phase used in combined training, eventing and horse trials.

cross-noseband a noseband with cross-over straps. See *grakle*.

croup the area between the loins and top of the tail.

croupade a high-school movement in which the hind legs leave the ground.

crupper a leather strap fitted to a saddle which passes in a loop under a horse's tail. It prevents the saddle sliding forwards.

cub   a young fox.

cubes   a balanced and concentrated feed, the contents of which may vary according to the manufacturers' formula.

cup   a metal or plastic holder fitted to a wing of a jump into which a pole, plank or gate is rested.

curb   **1** a sprain or swelling on the lower part of the hock joint or tendon; **2** a type of bit used in conjunction with a snaffle in a Weymouth or double bridle. (See illustration on page 24.)

curb chain   a metal chain which is fitted to the curb and Pelham bits and which lies in the groove of the lower jaw, above the lower lip. When pressure is applied through the curb reins, the curb chain tightens. Its use can be severe if it is not thoroughly understood and used with care.

curb reins   the reins attached to a curb bit. It is usual for curb reins to be made narrower than snaffle reins.

Curragh, the   the well-known racecourse in County Kildare, Ireland.

curricle   a two-wheeled vehicle pulled by a pair of horses driven abreast.

curry comb   a flat, square-shaped comb with a handle. Used for cleaning a body brush. (See illustration on page 56.)

cut   gelded.

cut and laid   a fence made by cutting thorn branches half-way through and binding them in and out through stakes set in the fence.

cutter   a type of sleigh designed with a high dash front which prevents snow being thrown back and over the passengers from the horses' hooves.

cutting horse   a horse trained for separating cattle. The name 'cutting horse' comes from the work it does – cutting out or cutting away and separating.

D

daisy cutter describes the action where a horse or pony walks or trots with little elevation.

Dales one of the nine British native pony breeds. The Dales have been bred and worked in the north-eastern part of England for centuries. For many years they were used to carry lead or coal from the mines to the ports and, like the Fell, have a quiet and calm temperament. They are exceptionally strong and sure-footed.

dam the female parent of a foal.

dandy brush a brush with long stiff bristles used for removing caked mud and surface dirt from a horse's coat and legs. It should not be used on a mane or tail.

Darley Arabian with the Byerley Turk and Godolphin Arabian, the Darley Arabian was one of the founding sires of the English Thoroughbred. He was brought to England in 1704 as a four-year-old by the British Consul in Aleppo, Mr Thomas Darley.

Darragh, Paul (Ireland) one of Ireland's top show jumpers, Paul was born in County Kildare.

Dartmoor one of the nine British native pony breeds, bred from stock which have traditionally roamed Dartmore in south-western England. Many studs of pure-bred and part-bred Dartmoor ponies can be found throughout the British Isles, Europe and North America. This excellent riding pony for children stands up to 12.2 hands, and is found in all colours other than piebald or skewbald.

Dartnall rein a type of plaited rein of soft cotton.

A day rug

day rug a woollen rug fitted with a buckle at the front and a fillet string which passes under the tail.

D-cheek snaffle a bit similar to the eggbutt snaffle, but having rings shaped in the form of a D rather than an oval. (See illustration page 19.)

Derby, the one of the best-known horseraces in the world. The Derby Stakes are run at Epsom Downs in Surrey in June. The race, for three-year-old colts and fillies, was first run in 1780 and is over a distance of 2.4 kilometres (1½ miles). Colts carry 9st (57.15 kg), fillies 8st 11 lbs (55.79 kg).

dished face the distinctive profile of the head of the Arabian and some other horses, when the forehead is convex and the line between the forehead and muzzle appears concave.

dishing a term describing the action of a horse or pony when it throws one or both front feet in an outward and forward movement.

dismounting to dismount, first remove both feet from the stirrups. Take the reigns gently in the left hand and place this on the neck of the horse or pony. At the same time put the right hand on to the pommel of the saddle. Apply a little pressure with the hands and arms and swing the right leg up and round the quarters and vault off. The landing should be made on the balls of the feet.

The correct way to dismount

The action of the dismount should be smooth and carried out in a brisk fashion. Never attempt to dismount by bringing the right leg in front of the body and over the neck of the horse or pony: this may look clever, but it can be most dangerous.

disobedience a word found especially in show-jumping and cross-country events to denote a refusal, resistance, run-out, turning a circle, stopping or napping. Any disobedient act is penalised according to the rules of the competition or class.

disunited a term to describe the sequence of the canter when it is not true or 'united'. See *united*.

dock **1** to cut part of a horse's tail bone – now illegal in Great Britain; **2** the fleshy part underneath the top of a horse's tail.

dog cart an all-round and versatile two- or four-wheeled vehicle found throughout the British Isles during the nineteenth century. A dog cart was used for many purposes apart from carrying sporting or hunting dogs.

dog fox a male fox.

donkey an ass.

donkey feet See *boxy feet*.

dorsal stripe a continuous black, brown or dun stripe running down the back of the horse from the mane to the tail. Commonly found in Scandinavian and north European breeds, and in many Highland ponies.

double, a see *combination*.

double bridle see *Weymouth*.

double oxer a spread fence, not a parallel, built with a single pole at the back and filled with brush. It is usual for an oxer to be designed in an ascending form, with the brush slightly higher than the front top pole or plank.

drag hunting hunting by following an artificial scent which is made by trailing strong-smelling sacking or other impregnated material over the ground.

draught horse a horse used for drawing a vehicle, the term being commonly associated with the heavy breeds. In the U.S. referred to as 'draft'.

drawing knife a tool used by a farrier.

draw rein attached to the girth and then passes through the rings of a bit. Not for young riders.

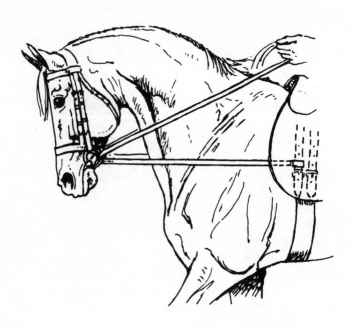

dray a low cart or wagon, without sides, used for carrying loads.

drench a medicine given as a drink, and sometimes mixed in water, linseed oil or castor oil.

dressage saddle see *saddle, dressage.*

driving hammer a tool used by a farrier.

drop fence an obstacle found in horse trials, cross-country events and hunting, where the land on the take-off side is higher than that found on the landing side.

drop noseband a type of noseband normally used with a snaffle, fitted around the muzzle and below the bit to prevent the horse opening its mouth. (See illustration on page 83.)

Dulmen a breed of pony living in semi-wild conditions in Westphalia, Germany. Height is up to 13 hands. All variety of colours are found.

dun a colour. There are two varieties of dun: yellow dun, which is between cream and golden-yellow in colour, and blue dun, a bluish-grey colour.

Dutch Heavy Draught a breed from Holland used extensively by farmers and market gardeners. The breed is of comparatively recent origin and is a calm, willing, active and honest worker. One of the heaviest of all draught horses.

E

earth   the underground home of a fox.

Edgar, Elizabeth (Great Britain)   a sister of David Broome and wife of Ted Edgar, Liz, as she is affectionately known, has enjoyed considerable success as a show jumper throughout the world.

Edgar, Ted (Great Britain)   for many years Ted Edgar has been one of Great Britain's leading show-jumping personalities. A brilliant rider and a great favourite with the crowd.

Edwards, Lionel   a well-known sporting artist and prolific illustrator of books. Born 1878: died 1976.

eggbutt   a type of snaffle bit, designed to avoid pinching of the lips. The eggbutt has a jointed mouthpiece and egg-shaped rings. (See illustration on page 19.)

elbow   the upper joint of the foreleg.

elimination   a competitor will be eliminated if, for any reason, he infringes those rules of the competition for which the penalty is that he should leave the ring. In show-jumping, one of many ways a competitor will be eliminated is by having accumulated three disobediences in any round.

equestrian   relates to horses or horsemanship. A person who rides.

equine   a horse, or of a horse.

equine influenza   a contagious and infectious virus which can be of epidemic proportions and afflict horses or ponies of any age, at any time. A yearly vaccination against the virus is the best protection.

Equus caballus the Latin name given to the domesticated horse.

ergot a horny growth found at the back of the fetlock joint.

ermine marks the black or brownish marks on white found in the area around the coronet of the hoof.

event **1** a class or competition held at a horse show; **2** a special competition, spread over one, two or three days, during which competitors will undertake two or three separate competitions including dressage, cross-country and show-jumping, and where the cumulative scores are used to determine the placings.

ewe neck where the crest, between the poll and the withers, slopes inwards and is concave rather than convex. Sometimes called an 'upside-down neck.'

exercise bandages the bandages fitted to support the tendons of the legs.

Exmoor one of the nine British native pony breeds. Exmoors are the oldest of the British pony breeds and inhabit the wild, high moorland in the south-west of England, from where they take their name. They are strong and most reliable, and are excellent as children's riding ponies. Exmoors are most hardy and can carry quite heavy weights for long periods. Height: up to 12.2 hands. Colours: bay-brown or dun, with characteristic 'mealy' colouring round the eyes, nose and often under the belly and on the inside of the legs.

extension when a horse or pony is asked by a rider to lengthen his stride. See *canter, extended* and *trot, extended* and *walk, extended*.

extravagant action an action which is high at the knee and hock, such as that given by the Hackney.

F

FBHS   Fellow of the British Horse Society.

FEI   Fédération Equestre Internationale – the international governing body of equestrian sport.

FRCVS   Fellow of the Royal College of Veterinary Surgeons.

Falabella   the smallest recorded horse in the world, which originated in the Argentine in South America. It stands not more than 76 cm (30 in), and its height is always given in centimetres or inches, not in hands and inches.

fall   a horse is considered to have fallen in a competition when the shoulders and quarters on the same side touch the ground. Different penalties are awarded against a fall depending on whether it is in a show-jumping competition or a horse trials' cross-country phase. A rider is said to have fallen when he has to remount.

family pony   a type of pony, particularly versatile and of good temperament and ability, which might be used by all members of one family.

farrier   a blacksmith. A craft member of the Worshipful Company of Farriers who removes, makes and fits shoes to horses and ponies.

fault   a fault in a jumping competition is any misdemeanour by a horse or pony or rider for which penalties are awarded. In show jumping four faults are awarded against any horse or rider who knocks down a fence or who dislodges any part of a fence in the act of jumping.

Any refusal, fall of horse or rider, or other disobedience is also penalised. (See *disobedience*.) A list containing the common faults in show jumping, together with a comprehensive list showing disobediences, is found in the *Rule Book* of the British Show Jumping Association, the sport's national governing body.

feather   the hair around the fetlock which is profuse in some breeds such as the Shire.

feeding, rules for good   the nine simple rules for good feeding are: **1** feed little and often; **2** wherever possible allow some grazing during the course of each day; **3** each day ensure plenty of bulk food, such as hay; **4** preferably feed at the same time every day; **5** always feed good, clean forage; **6** do not make sudden changes to the type of feed being given. If change is necessary, introduce it gradually; **7** never ask a horse or pony to undertake any work immediately after a feed; **8** water before feeding, but always keep a supply of fresh water available in a stable or field; **9** feed according to the work being done.

Fell   one of the nine British native pony breeds. The Fell ponies, like the Dales, are found in northern England and were used to carry lead and coal from the mines to the ports on the north-eastern coastline. Height is up to 14 hands, and they are mostly black, brown and grey, preferably with no white markings.

fence   see *obstacle*.

fetlock   the tuft of hair growing behind a fetlock joint. (See *points of the horse*, illustrated on page 93.)

fetlock joint   the joint between the lower part of the cannon bone and long pastern bone.

filly   a female horse under the age of four years.

firing   the application of a form of heat therapy or treatment which is carried out to the skin, tendons, ligaments and bones.

first pony   a type of pony suited to a beginner or younger rider. A first pony should always be one that is reliable and experienced, preferably with a known dependable temperament. See also *schoolmaster*.

Fjord a breed of pony native to Norway. Used widely for agricultural work in that country and in other parts of Scandinavia. Dun or cream in colour, they are small (up to 14 hands), adaptable, willing and hardworking.

flags used in show jumping, cross-country and hunter trials to indicate the extremities of the obstacle. When jumping the red flag is always to the right, and the white flag to the left.

flank the part of the horse behind the ribs and below the loins reaching down to the belly.

flash a broad white stripe running down a horse's face.

flash noseband a cavesson noseband with the addition of two straps which are sewn at the centre and cross over. This noseband, like the grakle, fastens below the bit, and is used with a standing martingale. (See illustration on page 83.)

flea-bitten a grey coat covered with hairs of a darker colour.

flecked a term used where collections or groupings of white hairs appear on any part of a horse's body.

Fletcher, Graham (Great Britain) born in Yorkshire, Graham Fletcher is one of the outstanding international riders competing today.

flexion a horse or pony yielding or giving its mouth to the pressures applied through the bit is said to have flexion.

floating a word used in the United States for tooth rasping.

flying change a change of the leading leg at the canter, when the horse has all four legs in the air.

foal a colt, gelding or filly up to the age of twelve months. A male foal is a colt foal; a female, a filly foal.

fodder foodstuffs fed to horses and ponies.

fodder room the place set aside for the storage of feed, which should be kept in vermin-proof bins.

foot follower   a person who follows a pack of hounds other than when mounted.

forage   another word meaning food.

forearm   the part of the foreleg between elbow and knee.

forehand   the neck, head, shoulders, withers and forelegs; in other words, all that part of a horse or pony which is in front of a rider.

foreleg   either of the front legs.

forelock   the part of a mane which extends between the ears and falls over the forehead.

four-in-hand   a team of four horses. The two in front are known as leaders; the two nearest the vehicle are the wheelers.

fox   any of certain carnivores of the dog family, especially those of the genus *Vulpes*. Smaller than wolves, the fox is characterised by a pointed muzzle, erect ears, and long bushy tail.

foxhound   one of a breed of hounds bred and trained for hunting the fox. Foxhounds are fleet and keen-scented, and stand between twenty-one and twenty-five inches at the shoulder.

foxglove   a plant found in many fields and hedgerows which is dangerous to horses and ponies when eaten in excess.

free walk   a term used in dressage where a horse is permitted to walk fully extended with complete freedom of head and neck. A walk not inhibited by 'strong' hands.

Friesian   a breed of heavy horse from Holland; an excellent, all-round harness horse and in use on both farms and in the cities. Standing about 15 hands, the Friesian is black, preferably without any markings or other colours.

frog   a part of the foot. A V-shaped pad of tissue situated between the bars on the underside of the foot, the point of which runs towards the toe. See illustration opposite.

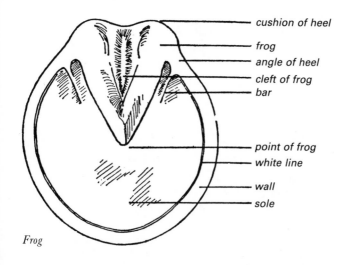

Frog

front   that part of a horse or pony which is in front of a rider. See *forehand*.

full brother or full sister   where foals have the same dam and sire.

full clip   when the entire coat is clipped out.

full horse   a horse not gelded.

fullered shoe   a shoe which has a groove round the ground surface where the nail holes are placed, which grips the ground and helps to make the shoe lighter.

full mouth   mouth of a horse at six years of age.

Fulmer snaffle   a snaffle bit with cheek-pieces attached to a jointed mouthpiece. (See illustration on page 19.)

furlong   a unit of distance used in racing, equivalent to 200 metres (220 yards).

G

gadfly   the gadfly, botfly or horsefly can be a particular problem in summer months. The eggs of the gadfly appear as small, yellow specks on the legs of horses and ponies and are licked and taken into the stomach. Not dangerous but should be treated immediately.

gag   the gag bridle acts to raise the head by lifting the bit against the corners of the mouth. It is used to control strong and impetuous horses.

gait   See *pace*.

gall   a skin sore, frequently caused by a badly fitted saddle or girth.

gallop   the fastest of the four natural paces.

Galvayne's mark or groove   a dark groove or mark appearing on the upper incisor teeth when the horse is about ten years of age. As the horse grows older the groove moves downwards, finally reaching the bottom of the teeth at the age of twenty years, after which it disappears.

gaskin   that part of a hindleg above the hock and reaching to the stifle.

gelding   a castrated male horse of any age.

general-purpose saddle   another name for an all-purpose saddle which can be used for all equestrian activities. See under *saddle*.

'getting underneath'   an expression in jumping where a horse or pony takes off too near the obstacle. The opposite is 'standing back' or taking off too soon.

gig   a two-wheeled vehicle designed and built for a

driver and one passenger. Used throughout the nineteenth century.

girth a band of leather, webbing or nylon, plain or plaited, which goes under the belly of a horse to hold a saddle in place.

girth straps the straps on a saddle to which a girth is attached.

give with the hand the act of opening the fingers sufficiently to relax the tension of the reins.

Godolphin Arabian one of the three founding sires of the English Thoroughbred, brought to England in 1732. See also *Darley Arabian* and *Byerley Turk*.

going a word indicating the condition and nature of the ground. 'Good going', 'soft going' and 'heavy going' are self-explanatory.

gone in the wind unsound in wind.

gone to ground a term used in hunting when the fox takes refuge in an earth or a drain.

good hands a rider's hands which are both light and sensitive.

goose rump a pronounced falling away of the hindquarters from the highest point toward the tail.

governess cart a two-wheeled vehicle, entered from the rear, and used at the turn of this century to carry a governess and children in her charge.

Grakle a cross or double noseband. (See illustration on page 83.)

grass-kept a horse or pony kept out at all times is known as being 'grass-kept'.

grazing suitable pastureland, meadow or grassland on which to put horses and ponies to feed.

grey (colour) a mixture of black and white hairs throughout an entire coat. In an 'iron' grey the black is most pronounced; in a light grey, white hairs are predominant. With age the shade of grey becomes lighter, but there is no white horse; even the lightest of colours is referred to as a grey.

groom   a person who looks after horses and ponies at the stable.

grooming   the five objects of grooming are: to promote health; to prevent disease; to maintain condition; to improve appearance, and to ensure cleanliness.

grooming kit   the basic equipment necessary for grooming includes a dandy brush, body brush, curry comb, hoof pick, sponges, stable rubber, water brush, mane comb, wisp.

dandy brush

body brush

rubber curry comb

wisp

sponge

hoof-pick

metal curry comb

comb

water brush

stable rubber

Grooming kit

groundline   a pole placed on the ground in front of an obstacle by which a horse or pony can judge the correct point of take-off. Shadows and ridges on the ground can cast a false groundline. This must be taken into account by the rider as the animal approaches an obstacle.

gymkhana   an event made up with different mounted games for younger riders, including musical sacks, bending races, potato races, and chase-me-charlies.

H

habit the dress worn by women when riding side-saddle.

HIS Hunters' Improvement Society.

hack a type of horse, not a breed; one suitable for riding. See *hunter, polo pony, cob*.

hack, to a general term used when 'going for a ride'.

hackamore see *bitless bridle*.

Hackney a high-stepping horse or pony with a characteristic and spectacular natural trot. The action of the horse is free, and gives an appearance of moving quickly across the top of the ground. Common colours are dark brown, bay and chestnut. The height for Hackney horses varies between 15 and 16 hands, and the ponies stand up to 14 hands.

Hackney coach a horse-drawn taxi first seen in London in the seventeenth century. Pulled by two horses, the coach had four wheels but no springing device, making it a most uncomfortable way of travelling.

Haflinger a breed from the south Austrian Tyrol. The Haflinger is a strong, sure-footed pony used for both agricultural work and as a pack pony. Height up to 13.3 hands.

half-breed a term used in describing a horse which has been bred from one of the parents being a Thoroughbred.

half-pass a movement in dressage in which the horse, facing ahead with the body parallel to the longer sides of an arena, moves sideways and forwards on two tracks, i.e. the hind legs follow a different track to the forelegs.

halt a position in which the horse or pony should stand square and still with the weight evenly distributed over each of the legs.

halter a rope or hemp headpiece for leading or tying-up. See also *head collar*.

hand the word used when measuring or giving the height of a horse or pony. A 'hand' is based on the width of a man's hand, estimated at 10 cm (4 in).

hands, good a rider said to have 'good hands' is one who is responsive and sympathetic to each movement of the horse or pony's head, giving and taking to each change of emphasis felt.

Hanoverian a strong, powerful German-bred horse which stands between 16 and 17 hands. Mostly found bay, brown, chestnut and black, the Hanoverian is very intelligent, bold and athletic. For many years this was a horse with many uses, but today the modern Hanoverian shows particular talent for show jumping and dressage.

Hansom the first hansom was built in 1830 and for many years was used as a taxi.

Haringey an arena in north London that was used for many years as the setting for major horse shows and displays.

harness a word which describes the equipment used in driving.

harness class a showing class for harness horses.

harness racing a form of horse racing in which the horse maintains a trotting pace while pulling a two-wheeled vehicle, known as a 'sulky' in which the driver is seated. Harness racing is very popular in the United States, Canada, Australia and some of the north-European countries.

haute école (high school) a training to the principles of the classic form of riding. The art of classical riding.

hay grass that has been cut and dried; the best substitute for natural grazing. Used throughout the year, it should be fed regularly to stable-kept horses and ponies and to those kept out in autumn and winter months. Hay is harvested during the early summer before the seeds have fallen. When handled it should have a sweet and pleasant aroma. Dry and dusty hay must be avoided, as should 'new' hay, that which has been cut in the previous six months.

hayloft   the area above a stable in which hay and other foodstuffs are stored.

hay net   a net (below) made from rope, hemp, jute or plastic into which hay is placed before feeding. Three sizes are available: a small net holding about 2 kg (4 lb); a medium net holding between 3.5 and 4 kg (8 and 9 lb) and a large net holding about 6.5 kg (14 lb).

head collar   a headpiece made in leather, hemp or

nylon without a bit. Used for leading and for tying-up. See *halter*.

head markings the markings on heads are 'natural' markings, and each has been given a name by which it can be identified. White marks on horses are described as: **1** *snip*, a white mark between the nostrils; **2** *star*, a white mark on the forehead; **3** *blaze*, a broad white mark running down the face, spreading as it nears the muzzle; **4** *stripe*, a narrow white line on the face; **5** *white face*, white covering the forehead and area around the eyes, nose and parts of the muzzle; **6** *wall eye*, see under *wall eye*.

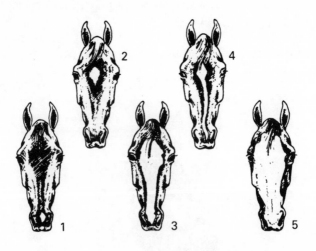

Head markings: 1 snip; 2 star; 3 blaze; 4 stripe; 5 white face

heavy horse any of the horses belonging to one of the breeds of large draught horses, including the Shire, Suffolk Punch, Clydesdale, Breton, Percheron and Dutch Draught Horse. There are twenty-three recognized breeds of heavy horse in the world.

height the height of a horse or pony is measured from

the ground to the highest part of the withers. When being measured, the animal must be standing square on level ground. One quarter of an inch (6 mm) is allowed should the horse or pony be shod.

Heins, Johan (Holland) the winner of the Men's European Championships in 1977, who has represented Holland on several occasions.

hemlock a plant found in some fields and hedgerows which is dangerous when eaten in excess.

Hickstead the site of the All-England Jumping Course in Sussex and one of the finest show jumping arenas in the world. Established in 1960 by Douglas Bunn, Hickstead has contributed much to a wider appreciation of show jumping.

Highland one of the nine British native pony breeds, the Highland comes from Scotland and the Western Isles. Sure-footed and kindly, it makes an ideal all-round pony. Height up to 14.2 hands. The breed produces a variety of colours, from dun through all shades of yellow to cream, bay, brown, black, chestnut and grey.

high school the classical art of equitation. See *haute école*.

hind leg a back leg.

Hobday an operation performed to treat 'roaring', an affliction of the horse's larynx.

hogged mane a mane of a horse or pony which has been clipped out or shaved off. In the United States this is called 'roaching' the mane.

hog's back a type of fence used in show jumping where the centre pole of three elements is higher than the one in front and the one behind. From a side view a hog's back looks somewhat like an upside-down V.

Holderness-Roddam, Jane (Great Britain) a winner of the Badminton Three-day Event and Burghley, Jane Holderness-Roddam has been one of the most consistent competitors since she began her riding career with show ponies at an early age.

holloa the cry or call given by a person who sights a fox.

Holstein a breed from Holstein in Germany, eminently suitable for all equestrian activities, including show jumping and cross-country riding. Stands between 15.2 and 16.2 hands.

hoof the foot.

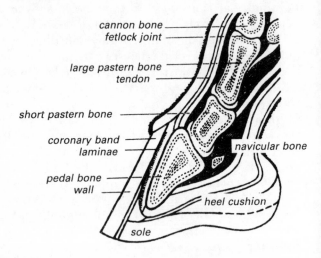

Parts of the foot or hoof

hoof oil an oil brushed on the feet after grooming to prevent brittle feet and to improve the general appearance.

hoof-pick a tool used in grooming. The hoof pick is a metal or plastic device used for cleaning mud, dirt and stones from horses' feet.

horn **1** the outer surface of the hoof. Also called the 'wall'; **2** a copper horn used by a huntsman, usually about 25.5 cm (10 in) in length; **3** a copper or brass horn used by coachmen.

'Horse and Hound' founded in 1884, the best-known and most widely read equestrian journal.

horse blanket   a thick, warm blanket used to supplement a night rug in cold weather.

horse-box   a vehicle designed specifically for the transport of horses and ponies.

horse brasses   the brass ornaments and fittings of many different shapes and designs affixed to the harness of working horses.

horse dealer   a person who buys and sells horses.

Horse of the Year Show   an indoor horse show organised by the British Show Jumping Association. Taking place each October, the show is one of the major events in the British calendar. Since 1959 the Horse of the Year Show has been held at Wembley, London.

horse race   a race for horses ridden by jockeys over a measured distance. Horse races can be over a 'flat' course, where no obstacles are presented, or over hurdles or steeplechase fences. Some races are handicapped, and the weight carried is adjusted to take into account previous performance. The Rules governing racing in Great Britain are administered by the Jockey Club based at Newmarket.

horse sale   the traditional place at which to buy and sell. Horse sales are advertised from time to time in the local papers and the specialist equestrian press.

horseshoe   the metal shoe or plate which is fitted to all horses and ponies who are in work. Horseshoes can be made and fitted by one of two methods: cold shoeing or the traditional hot shoeing. When cold shoeing is used a previously made and shaped shoe is fitted to the horse after minor adjustments are made to ensure fit. In the hot shoeing process a shoe is specifically made in a forge, shaped and adjusted as necessary, before being fitted.

horse trailer   an independent trailer designed to be towed by a vehicle and which can hold one, two or three horses or ponies.

hunt, to   the activity of pursuing a fox or hare by following hounds.

hunter   a type of horse, not a breed of horse. See also *hack, cob, polo pony*.

hunter classes   the name given to competitions held at horse shows to determine the best at each of the 'weights' and usually a champion and reserve champion from all of the 'weights'. Among the headings for such classes are: Lightweight hunters, Middleweight hunters, Heavyweight hunters, Ladies' Show hunters, and Small Show hunters.

hunter clip   a clip similar to a full clip, but some hair is left on the legs as far as the elbows and thighs, and a patch in the shape of a saddle is left on the back.

hunter trials   a type of competition, mostly staged by hunts during the season, in which horses are ridden over a course of natural-looking obstacles. A hunter trials' course is measured and a time is determined. Faults, other than those received by disobedience, falls, etc. on the course, are added when the time taken from start to finish exceeds the 'bogey' or set time.

hunting tie   see *stock*.

huntsman   the person in charge of hounds during a hunt.

hurdles   in hurdle racing the minimum number of the hurdles to be jumped is six flights in the first 1½ miles, and one hurdle for every additional ¼ mile or less.

I

Icelandic a most adaptable breed of pony possibly originating from Norwegian and Shetland stock. The Icelandic pony is short and sturdy (between 12 and 13 hands) and is a rugged, intelligent and hardy breed.

impulsion the energy built up in the horse's quarters and hocks. It is this energy or impulsion which is controlled by the rider's hands through the bit.

in-breeding the mating of a brother and sister, sire and daughter or dam and son.

incisors the front, or biting, teeth.

in foal said of a mare when pregnant.

in front of the bit an expression used where a horse or pony takes too much hold and pulls.

in hand the term used for a horse or pony being led.

A horse being shown 'in hand'

Irish Draught a breed of horse, standing between 15 and 16.1 hands, the result of a cross between the Thoroughbred and native Irish mares. The breed is sturdy and honest and is used for all equestrian activities. Often seen in the hunting field.

Irish rings a type of martingale. See illustration page 78.

'irons' a word used for stirrups.

J

Jack a male donkey.

Jenny a female donkey.

Jenny Lind a light four-wheeled American vehicle named after the famous Swedish singer.

jib a horse or pony is said to jib when it refuses to go forward and, in some cases, moves backwards or sideways.

jockey a rider, male or female, professional or amateur, engaged in horse-racing.

Jockey Club, the the governing body of horse-racing in the British Isles.

jodhpurs a form of breeches worn for riding.

jointed Pelham a Pelham bit with a jointed mouth-piece similiar to that found in a jointed snaffle.

jointed snaffle a bit with a jointed mouthpiece and circular or D-shaped rings.

judge a person appointed to make decisions in any competition and qualified to pass critical judgement.

jumping the wrong course an expression used where a competitor jumps, or attempts to jump, an obstacle in the wrong order, or who misses or avoids the correct obstacle and jumps or attempts to jump a fence out of sequence. The penalty for jumping, or taking the wrong course, is elimination.

jumping, the act of the four recognised stages in the act of jumping are: **1** the approach; **2** the take-off; **3** the suspension, and **4** the landing. (See the illustration on pages 68–9.)

jump off in show jumping, a jump-off is sometimes necessary to determine the winner and placings in competitions. A jump-off is timed and invariably takes place over a shortened course with obstacles raised in height. See *against the clock*.

jumps see *obstacles*.

jute rug a night rug made of jute.

Jumping: 1 *the approach;*   2 *the take-off*

3 *the suspension;*   4 *the landing*

K

Kellett, Iris (Ireland) once a member of Ireland's international team and winner in 1969 of the Ladies' European Championship.

kennels the buildings or yard which house a pack of hounds.

Kimblewick a combination of a snaffle and curb bit using a single rein. (See illustration on page 19.)

Kineton noseband a type of noseband which, by means of two semicircular leather-covered metal hoops, puts pressure on the horse's nose.

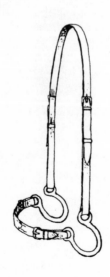

klibber   a woollen saddle made for Shetland ponies.

Knabstrup   a spotted breed from Denmark. Standing between 15.2 and 16 hands they were popular as circus horses. Mostly white with black or brown spots over the head, body and legs.

knacker's yard   the place where horses are slaughtered.

knee caps   felt pads buckled on to protect horses' knees when exercising or travelling. See illustration below.

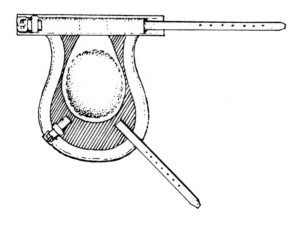

knee-roll   a pad at the front part of the flap of a saddle in front of the rider's knee.

knock-down   an expression used when a pole or any part of any obstacle in the vertical plane in jumping falls or is displaced through a fault by a horse or rider. The penalty for a knock-down when show jumping is four faults, but should a knock-down occur in the act of a disobedience, the rider will be stopped by the judge and time penalties will also be added.

L

laburnum a plant found in many fields and hedgerows which is dangerous to horses and ponies if eaten in excess.

laminitis a painful inflammation or fever of the feet, usually brought about by fast work on hard ground, too much rich grass or heating food. Laminitis may also arise when there is insufficient exercise.

landing side the far side of an obstacle.

laurel a shrub found in many fields and hedgerows which is dangerous to horses and ponies if eaten in excess.

leaders the name given to the front pair of horses in a team of four. Those nearer the carriage are known as wheelers.

leading rein **1** a rope or webbing strap used to lead a horse or pony; **2** a showing class for competitors who are led throughout the competition, usually for very young riders as an introduction to equestrian sport.

leathers, stirrup the straps which attach to the saddle and which hold the stirrup irons.

leaving the ring a horse or rider who leaves the ring without permission of the judges is eliminated from that competition.

left behind an expression where a rider is thrown back in the saddle as the horse or pony jumps instead of having adjusted his weight and centre of gravity by moving forward with the action of the horse.

leg markings the names given to markings on the

horse's legs. These are named after the area they cover, e.g. a white stocking extends to the knee or hock; a white sock covers the fetlock and part of the cannon bone area; white fetlock, white pastern and white coronet are self-explanatory.

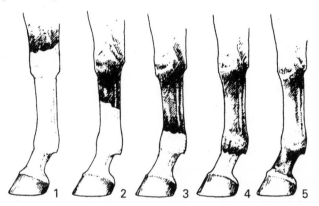

Leg markings: 1 stocking; 2 sock; 3 fetlock; 4 pastern; 5 coronet

leg up   the assistance given by another person to the rider when mounting.
Liberty horses   circus horses.
light of bone   a horse is said to be light of bone when the measurement of the bone immediately below the knee is insufficient. Sometimes referred to as 'short of bone'.
linseed   the seed of flax and high in protein value. Before being used in any feed linseed must be boiled to soften the seeds.
linseed mash   a nutritious feed made from linseed and bran, which can be made by taking 0.5 litres (1 pint) of linseed allowing this to soak in cold water for about two hours. Mix with bran and bring to the boil. Let it simmer for three or four hours. Feed once the mash or gruel is cool, but do not use it if it has stood for more than twenty-hour hours.

linseed tea   another way of giving linseed to horses and ponies. To make the tea, take 1 litre (2 pints) of linseed and boil it in 9 litres (2 gallons) of water. When the seeds are soft, the highly nutritious water can be taken and used as an additive to a feed.

Lipizzaner   a breed which takes its name from Lipizza, the site of the original stud farm in Yugoslavia. World-renowned for their performances at the Spanish Riding School in Vienna, Lipizzaners are also used as coach horses and in agriculture.

lipstrap   a thin leather strap to keep a curb chain in place.

litter   the bedding material used in stables.

livery   a horse kept at the owner's expense at a place other than his home. A livery yard or stable undertakes to feed, groom and exercise the horses stabled at livery.

loins   the area between the back and the croup.

long reining   a method of schooling in which the trainer uses two reins which have been attached to the rings of a bit. The trainer walks behind the horse, using the reins to encourage and direct. Long reining is not advised for the younger or inexperienced person.

loose box   a stable, or area where horses and ponies can be kept, the size of which should never be less than 3 × 3.65m (10 × 12ft).

loose rein   a rein which hangs loosely, resting without a positive contact between the bit and rider's hands.

Loriner   a manufacturer of bits, spurs, stirrups and other metal devices used in riding.

Loriston-Clarke, Jennie   (Great Britain) Britain's finest exponent of dressage and an all-round horsewoman. Winner of many national and international competitions.

'lost a pedal'   an expression used when a rider's foot is not resting in the stirrup iron.

lungeing   the act of using lunge reins to assist in making a horse more supple and obedient. Lungeing should only be undertaken by a younger rider when a person with experience is there to help.

lunge rein   a man-made fibre or webbing rein attached to a horse by means of a specially made cavesson noseband. (See illustration on page 30.) Used in schooling and training.

lungeing whip   an essential part of lungeing equipment. Made of cane with a long, light thong, the lungeing whip is rarely lifted from the ground, and is held in the hand which is not holding the lunge rein.

M

MFH Master of Foxhounds.

MRCVS Member of the Royal College of Veterinary Surgeons.

Mac, Michael (Great Britain) the 1980 Junior European Champion.

Macken, Eddie (Ireland) among the world's most popular riders, Eddie Macken was born in County Longford in Ireland and for many years has remained at the top of the show-jumping tree.

'made' a horse or pony is claimed to have been 'made' when its breaking or initial training is complete.

Madison Square Garden an indoor arena in New York, used each year to stage horse shows and other equestrian events.

mane the long hair which grows from the top of a horse's head, down the neck and crest to the withers.

mane comb a long-toothed plastic or metal comb used to clean or 'pull' a mane.

manège an enclosure for schooling a horse or pony.

manger a container to hold feedstuff fixed to the wall in a stable or loose box.

mare a female horse of four years or over.

Market Harborough the Market Harborough is a type of martingale, though it is referred to as a rein. Under BSJA rules a gag snaffle and a Market Harborough rein may be used, but running or check reins of any other kind are not permitted. A Market Harborough may at such times be used only with a snaffle. (See illustration overleaf.)

markings see *leg markings* and *head markings*.

martingale an artificial aid used to regulate the head carriage of a horse or pony. A martingale is a strap, one end of which is attached to the noseband, reins or bit (depending which type of martingale is used), the other end to the girth. Another strap round the horse's neck holds it in place. (See illustration overleaf.)

McMahon, Paddy (Great Britain) a consistent and hardworking rider who has represented Great Britain many times in international competitions. He rode Pennwood Forge Mill to win the 1973 Men's European Championship.

measuring stick a device made from wood with an adjustable arm to rest on the highest part of the withers. The stick stands on the ground and the height is determined by the reading given when the arm rests on the withers at a right-angle.

medicine cabinet a fully stocked medicine cabinet or chest is an essential part of any stable yard. It should be kept at hand and replenished when items have been used. The contents of a cabinet might include: calico bandages; rolls of cotton wool; packets of lint; a roll or two of gamgee or other tissue; packets of oiled silk; one or two colic drinks from a veterinary surgeon, though these should not be kept for too long; a bottle of embrocation; witch hazel; kaolin; methylated spirits; Epsom salts and a bottle of glycerine. It is also important to keep in the medicine cabinet a pair of blunt-ended 10-cm (4-in) scissors.

metacarpal bone the common bone and the main bone of the front leg.

metatarsal bone the cannon or shank bone, the main bone of the hind leg.

milk teeth the name given to the horse's first teeth found at or shortly after birth.

molars the large grinding teeth found beyond the bars

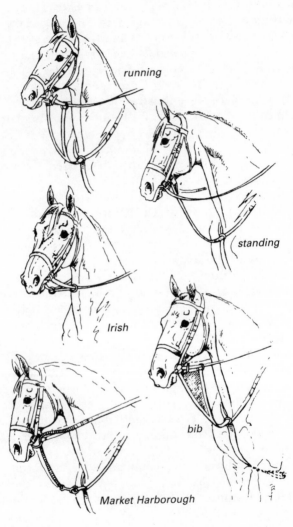

running

standing

Irish

bib

Market Harborough

Martingales

of the mouth and behind the incisor teeth.

molasses a sweetener loved by horses and ponies when used as an additive to normal 'dry' feeds. Molasses are made from uncrystallised syrup drained from raw sugar. The syrup should be mixed with hot water before adding to a feed.

Morgan a breed of light horse originating from the Vermont district of the United States. Named after Justin Morgan, the man who bred the original horses, this is a versatile, honest and kindly horse, widely used in all riding activities. The Morgan stands between 14 and 15.2 hands.

Mould, Marion (Great Britain) the winner of the Ladies' World Championship in 1965 and a most consistent and successful rider, perhaps best known and remembered for the years she competed with Stroller. Has represented Great Britain on many occasions.

mountain and moorland ponies the group of the nine British native pony breeds which take their names from that part of the country in which they have their origin, i.e Shetland, Highland, Fell, Dales, Welsh, New Forest, Dartmoor, Exmoor and Connemara.

mounting to mount, first check that the girth is tight and the stirrup irons are let down. Stand with the left shoulder to the horse's near side and take the reins in the left hand. Place the left hand in front of the withers and, with the right hand holding the stirrup, place the left foot in the iron. Press down the toe and face the horse. Take hold of the waist on the far side of the saddle and spring up, swinging the right leg over the quarters (taking care not to kick the horse) and come to rest quietly into the saddle. Place the right foot in the stirrup and take up the reins with both hands.

mouth, a full the term used when a horse's milk teeth have been replaced by permanent teeth, usually reached when a horse is five years old.

mucking-out a daily routine during which stained

bedding is removed.

mud fever an inflammation of the legs and belly caused by mud and extreme wet conditions.

mule the offspring of a male donkey and female horse.

Munnings, Sir Alfred a well-known equestrian artist. Born 1878: died 1959.

music the sound made by hounds when hunting.

muzzle 1 the part of the head including the nostrils, lips and teeth; 2 a device put over a horse's mouth to prevent the horse from biting or from eating its bedding.

N

nag a poor quality horse.

napping when a horse refuses to go forward or respond to the aids given by the rider. A 'nappy' horse is one deemed to be resisting (see page 100) and is penalised in jumping competitions as for a disobedience.

native breeds the name given to any breed coming or originating from a particular place or country. Native ponies include the nine British native pony breeds (see under *mountain and moorland*); there are also several British native breeds of horses, including the Shire, Suffolk Punch, Clydesdale, etc. The Breton, Fjord, Icelandic, Hanoverian and Lipizzaner also come under the heading of native breeds.

natural aids the aids given by a rider by the use of his hands, body, legs and voice.

navicular bone a small bone in the foot between the short pastern bone and the pedal bone.

navicular disease a disease found in the fore-feet caused by weakness or too much work suddenly undertaken after a period of rest. There is no known cure for this disease.

near fore the left foreleg.

near hind the left hind leg.

near side the left-hand side of a horse or pony.

neck-reining the act of steering or guiding a horse by applying pressure against the neck with the reins on the side opposite to the direction in which it is required to move.

Newbury, Tony (Great Britain)   a regular competitor at international events and member of Great Britain's Olympic Team in 1976.

New Forest   one of the nine British native pony breeds, the New Forest originates from Hampshire in southern England. An excellent pony for children – honest, quiet, kindly and obedient, and useful for all different aspects of riding and sport. Colours can be any other than piebald or skewbald. Height: up to 14.2 hands.

Newmarket   the horse-racing centre in the United Kingdom. Established in 1665 and the headquarters of the Jockey Club, the governing body of racing and Thoroughbred breeding in Britain.

New Zealand rug   a stout, lined waterproof rug giving excellent protection during winter months for clipped or thin-coated horses out at grass. Used, in one form or another, throughout the world. The rug is fitted by attaching two straps around the hind legs, and a single strap across the breast.

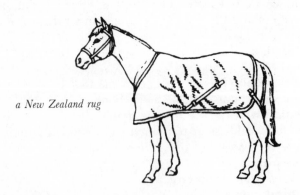

a New Zealand rug

night rug   a rug made from jute or canvas and sometimes lined with a woollen blanket. Of the many different types of rugs in use, the night rug is perhaps the most essential and useful. Night rugs are needed to keep clipped horses warm in the stable in winter.

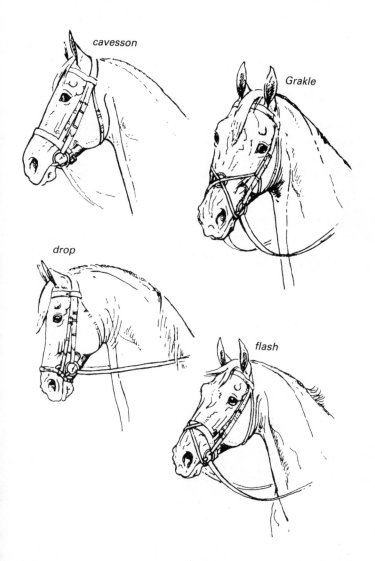

Nosebands (see overleaf)

83

Norfolk cart   a two-wheeled cart used for similar purposes as a dog cart, with back-to-back seating for four people.

noseband   a part of most bridles. The cavesson, drop, flash, Kineton and Grakle are some of the nosebands in use today. A noseband must be fitted correctly since it forms an integral part of bitting. See illustration page 83.

novice   an inexperienced horse or pony or rider.

numnah   a cotton, felt, sheepskin or nylon pad in the shape of, and worn under, a saddle.

nutcracker   a horse which has acquired the habit of grinding its teeth.

O

Oaks a horse-race over 1 mile 4 furlongs held each year since 1779 at Epsom in Surrey for three-year-old fillies.

oats a foodstuff, the best of which are the short, plump variety which have a sweet taste and pleasant smell. Oats give energy, and because of this great care must be taken when feeding them to ponies being ridden by younger children or inexperienced riders. A wrongly balanced diet, or too much oats, may make a pony over-full of himself and virtually uncontrollable.

obstacle a fence or jump used in show jumping, at horse trials or at practice.

obstacles, types of the basic types or shapes of the obstacles to be found in the show-jumping arenas are: the upright or vertical; the parallel; the ascending spread; the triple bar or staircase type; and the hog's back. From these shapes a course designer or course builder can create a wide variety of interesting and testing jumps. (See illustrations overleaf.)

odd coloured an expression used where the colour of a horse or pony cannot be described as one of the recognised or accepted colours.

off fore the right foreleg.

off hind the right hind leg.

offside the right-hand side of a horse or pony.

Ogilvie, William Henry a prolific writer of sporting verse. Born 1869: died 1963.

Oldenburg the heaviest of the German warm-bloods.

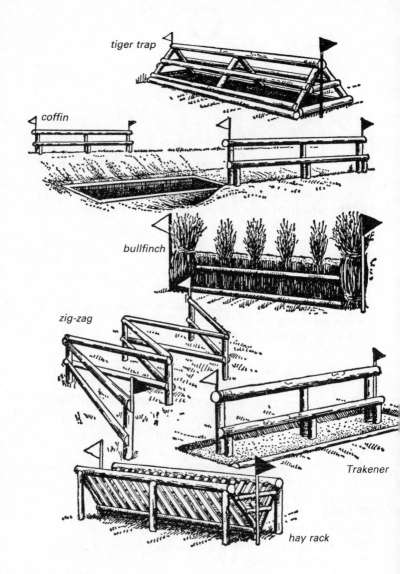

Some obstacles – Horse Trials

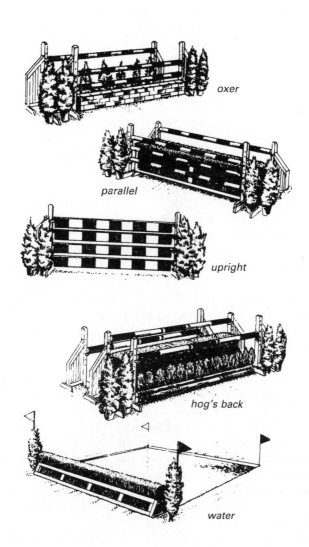

oxer

parallel

upright

hog's back

water

Some obstacles – the Show Ring

Frequently standing at 17 hands, they are mostly found black, brown or bay. The Oldenburg is a steady and bold horse, used widely as a coach horse, though is now widely used as a riding horse.

Oliver, Alan (Great Britain) for many years Alan Oliver represented Great Britain in international show-jumping competitions throughout the world. Today he is much sought after as a course designer and course builder.

Olympia a venue in London at which is staged the International Horse Show each Christmas time. The home of the International Horse Show from 1907 to 1939.

Olympic Games the three equestrian activities at the Olympic Games are dressage, show jumping and a three-day event.

on the bit a horse or pony is 'on the bit' when a rider can feel through the reins that he is in contact with the horse through the bit.

one-day event an equestrian competition completed during one day, during which competitors face three sections: dressage, cross-country and show jumping.

outside assistance after a signal to start has been given by a judge a competitor in an affiliated show-jumping competition will be eliminated if any outside assistance is received, whether that assistance was asked for or not. Not counting as outside assistance for the purpose of this rule: catching loose horses; assisting to mount; repairing broken tack after a fall; medical or veterinary assistance; picking up and handing back glasses or head gear.

over-face, to a horse or pony is over-faced when asked to tackle obstacles which are far beyond his capability. The opposite of over-face is under-face.

over-reach boot a protective boot made from rubber or plastic designed to prevent damage caused by over-reaching.

over-reaching   the injury or damage caused when the rim or edge of a hind shoe strikes the heel of a foot in front.

oxer   an obstacle in show jumping which is built as an ascending fence with brush placed between the front line of poles or planks and the single back pole. (See illustration on page 87.)

P

pace or gait. A horse or pony normally will have four paces if one accepts the gallop as being separate from a fast canter: they are the walk, trot, canter, gallop. The Americans have in addition the amble and show gait.

paddock a grass field, pasture land or enclosed area of grazing in which horses and ponies can be turned out.

Palomino a colour type of horse or pony, having a cream-coloured coat with flaxen, almost white mane and tail.

panel of a saddle the padded part lying under the saddle flap which rests against a horse's back.

parabola the arc made through the air in the act of jumping from the point of take-off to landing.

parallel a spread obstacle with a single pole as the back element. The parallel is considered to be the most difficult of fences, since the back pole is not immediately visible to a horse or pony at the moment of take-off. The fence must be jumped with precision, and the rider should treat it as an ascending spread, giving a horse every opportunity to clear the back pole.

parrot mouth a horse is said to have a 'parrot mouth' when the teeth of the lower jaw are set behind those of the upper jaw.

part-bred a horse or pony that has some relationship to a recognised breed. In some cases such animals are accepted by the Breed Society for inclusion in their specially kept part-bred register.

parts of a double bridle (See illustration on page 24).

90

passage a collected trot in a rhythm which appears to give the horse and rider a delayed suspension. It is a movement in dressage.

pastern the part of a horse's leg between the fetlock joint and the hoof.

Pegasus the winged white horse of ancient Greek mythology.

Pelham a bitting device which, like the Weymouth and double bridle, uses two sets of reins. The Pelham combines the actions of a snaffle and curb though one mouthpiece. (Illustrated on page 19.)

Pelham bridle the type of bridle used with a Pelham bit.

Percheron a 'clean-legged' heavy horse originating from the area of La Perche in the southern part of Normandy in France. This strong, willing and hardy horse is found in many countries of the world. The accepted colours are grey and black with little white hair.

pferd the German word for horse.

Phaeton a popular four-wheeled vehicle which first appeared in the latter part of the eighteenth century.

phenylbutazone a pain-killer, commonly referred to as 'bute'.

Phillips, Captain Mark (Great Britain) a brilliant horseman, both in three-day events and major show jumping competitions. Three times winner of Badminton (1971, 1972, 1974), Mark Phillips has also won at the Burghley Horse Trials, and received an Olympic gold medal as a member of the successful team in 1972.

piaffe a high-school movement in which a horse performs a passage (see above) on the spot, without a forward or backward movement.

piebald a horse or pony with large, irregular patches of black and white on the body.

pincers a tool used by a farrier.

pin firing see *firing*.

Pinto   a breed of horse found in the United States. Four distinct types are recognised – the *stock* type, the *hunter* type, a *pleasure* type, and a *saddle* type. The word 'pinto' comes from the Spanish word meaning paint, and the colouring is very similar to that found on piebalds and skewbalds, i.e. large white patches on a black or brown coat.

pirouette   a dressage movement in which a horse turns a full circle, pivoting on one hind leg.

plaits   the mane is plaited to show to advantage the neck and crest (called braiding in the United States). It is a common practice to have an odd number of plaits along the neck with an extra one hanging over the forehead.

plates   the word for the shoes worn by racehorses.

point-to-point   originally a race for horses between the point of one church steeple and that of another. Since 1945, however, point-to-point meetings have become popular events in the sporting calendar. Most hunts throughout Great Britain organise a point-to-point meeting, with only amateur riders competing, during the season which extends from February through to May.

points of the horse   the names given to the different parts of a horse's body. (See illustration opposite.)

poll   the area of a horse's head between its ears.

polo   a ball game played with sticks between two teams each of four mounted players. A polo ground measures 275 m (300 yd) by 145m (160 yd). The game, one of the oldest known in the world, is played in a series of 'chukkas', each timed to last for seven minutes. Players are allowed to change ponies after each chukka. At the end of a chukka there is an interval of three minutes with a five-minute interval at half-time.

polo pony   a type of pony used in the game of polo. Polo ponies are not a breed; they are a type, as are hunters, cobs and hacks.

polo stick   a long-handled mallet used in polo.

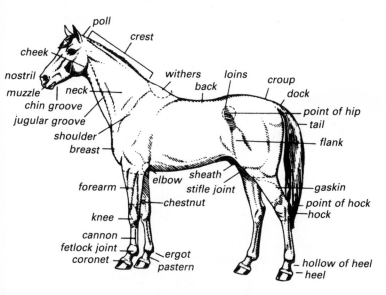

Points of the horse

pommel   the point at the front of a saddle.

pony   the most commonly accepted height limit for a pony is up to 14.2 hands, but this is not always the case. For example, a Hackney pony must not exceed 14 hands, and an Arab horse is always referred to as a 'horse' though it may stand under 14.2 hands. Polo ponies have no height restriction, and in some showing classes 'ponies' are accepted up to 15 hands.

pony cart   a four-wheeled vehicle or carriage built to be pulled by a single pony in harness. Widely used in Great Britain at the turn of the century.

Pony Club   an organisation founded in 1929 to encourage young people to ride and enjoy equestrian sport. Membership is open to all under 17 years and Associate Membership between 17 and 20 years. There are more than 130,000 members spread throughout the world, and the Pony Club is recognised as having the largest membership of any association of riders.

pony nuts   a manufactured feedstuff in a concentrated form. Since not all brands have similar ingredients it is sensible to check with the chandler or supplier to establish the nutritious value and content of any particular type of nuts.

post-and-rail   the best and safest type of fencing for paddocks and fields in which horses or ponies are kept.

Prince of Wales spur   a spur with a sloping neck which must lie pointing downwards when fitted.

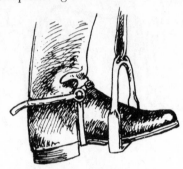

Prior-Palmer, Lucinda (Great Britain)   the world's leading lady three-day event rider, having won four times at Badminton. Also winner of several major international competitions.

pritchel   a pointed metal tool used by a farrier.

privet   a plant found in hedgerows which is dangerous to horses and ponies when eaten in excess.

Prix Caprilli   though taking place in a dressage area, Prix Caprilli is a test judged on riding ability.

puissance   a show-jumping competition in which the obstacles are reduced in number, raised and spreads widened, after each round. Only those horses going clear go forward to the next round, and the winner is the competitor with the least number of faults in the final round. When the height of the obstacles reaches a limit, or there have been three jumps-off, the judges may decide to share the placings.

94

pulled mane   a mane is tidied by removing or 'pulling' the hair with a mane comb.

pulled tail   the removal of hairs from the tail as mentioned above, done to neaten the appearance of the top of the tail.

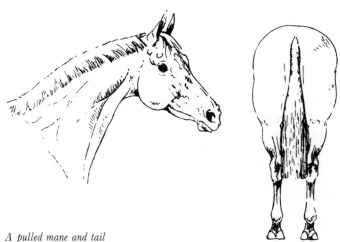

A pulled mane and tail

pulse   a horse's pulse is normally 36 to 40 beats to the minute.

pure-bred   a horse or pony with no mixed blood.

'putting to'   a term in driving when putting a horse or team of horses into a vehicle or carriage.

putting up a bridle or saddle   the expression used when a bridle or saddle is ready to hang in the tack room on a specially made rack.

Pyrah, Malcolm   a member of the British team which won the World Championship in 1978 and the European Team Championship in 1979. He has represented his country on several occasions. Pyrah was awarded the British Equestrian Federation Medal of Honour in 1980 for his services to the sport.

Q

quadrille   a display to music by four riders.

Quarter horse   an American-bred horse known for its ability to run at great speed over a straight quarter-mile track. Now used for other equestrian activities, though its fame spread as a first-class breed of racehorse.

quartering   a quick form of grooming sometimes carried out early in the morning when time does not allow a full grooming. If quartering is undertaken a full grooming is essential before the end of the day.

quarters   the part of a horse's body between the rear of the flank and root of the tail, stretching down to the top of the gaskin.

quarter sheet   a rectangular sheet or rug used on racehorses in the paddock or when at exercise. In the paddock it is held in place by a lightweight roller and breast strap; at exercise the front corners are folded back under the girth straps. Used in this way it is sometimes called a galloping sheet.

R

RDA   Riding for the Disabled Association.

racing silks   the colours of a racehorse owner which are worn by a jockey.

rack   an artificial gait in which each foot hits the ground separately. To 'rack up' means to tie up a horse or pony.

ragwort   a common plant which is highly dangerous when eaten in excess. Like most poisonous plants it should be dug from the ground and burned.

Ralli cart   a two-wheeled vehicle with curved sides first used at the end of the nineteenth century.

rapping   The act of rapping is where a horse or pony is asked to attempt to jump a pole which, at the last moment, is raised so that the pole is hit and the horse is thus encouraged to jump higher. Under FEI and BSJA rules rapping is not permitted. The BSJA rule states that no member shall allow a horse to be rapped or jump a rail or obstacle which is held by hand.

rasp   **1** a tool used by a farrier; **2** an instrument used by a veterinary surgeon for filing down teeth.

rasping   ragged edges of hoof are smoothed by rasping, and the word is also used to describe the removal of the sharp edges of molar teeth. In the United States, the word 'floating' is used with reference to teeth instead of rasping.

rearing   a horse or pony which stands up on its hind legs is rearing, and this, under the Rules of the British Show Jumping Association, constitutes a disobedience

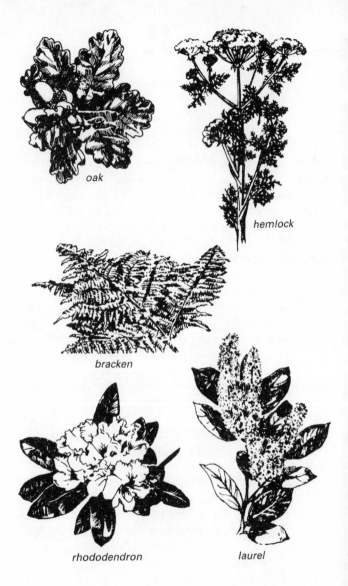

Some plants which are dangerous to horses and ponies when eaten in excess

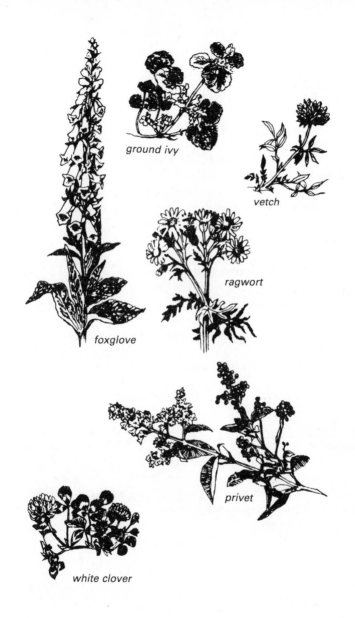

ground ivy

vetch

foxglove

ragwort

privet

white clover

and is penalised. Rearing is a most dangerous vice and one which is not easily treated. Should it become a habit a complete examination of the horse should be carried out by a veterinary surgeon.

red flag   a red flag is fixed to the right-hand side of an obstacle and thus denotes the direction in which it should be jumped. See *flags*.

refusal   in jumping competitions the act of refusing is penalised as a disobedience.

rein back   a movement by which a horse or pony takes three or four even paces backwards. This must be carried out with a slow, positive action in response to correct use of a rider's hands and leg aids.

reins   the leather, cotton or webbing straps used by a rider to make contact with the horse or pony's mouth by linking the action of the fingers and hands to the bit.

resisting   a horse which refuses to go forward, stops, runs back, rears or circles is said to be resisting. In competitions, if, after re-taking the track towards an obstacle, the horse resists again, it is penalised as for a second disobedience. Should an obstacle, through resistance, take more than one minute to jump it is penalised by elimination from that competition.

rhododendron   a shrub found in fields and hedgerows which is dangerous when eaten in excess.

ribbons   rosettes.

riding clubs   there are more than 400 riding clubs spread throughout Great Britain. The Riding Clubs' Association is affiliated to the British Horse Society, and offers its members many riding and social activities.

ride into the ground   to ride a horse or pony to its absolute limit.

riding out   an expression meaning any form of non-competitive riding.

rig   a male horse which has been unsuccessfully castrated. Such animals may behave like stallions and be difficult to manage.

ringbone a growth on the bone in the area of the pastern causing lameness.

risen clench a clench which is risen is one which has come away from the wall of the foot. This sharp-pointed end of a clench can cause injury and must be dealt with immediately it is seen or felt.

rising a term used when discussing the age of a horse or pony. If a horse is nearly six years old he is said to be 'rising' six.

rising trot see *trot, rising*.

roan a colour which can be either bay, strawberry or blue. A bay roan has a bay-based body with some white hairs giving it a reddish overall appearance; a strawberry roan is basically chestnut with a mixture of white hairs; a blue roan has a black-brownish body with white hairs giving it a distinct blue appearance.

roarer a horse which makes a noise as it breathes or after exertion. This invariably is due to a respiratory problem.

roller a type of surcingle used to keep rugs in place. It is usually made from hemp or leather, fastened with two buckles. Most rollers have two pads fitted on the underside to give protection to the spine.

rosettes the specially shaped ribbons, of different colours, which are presented to the horse or pony. In most competitions in Great Britain red is for the winner, blue is for second, yellow for third and green for fourth. Most rosettes carry the name of the Show, and in special competitions it is likely the sponsor of the class will also provide a commemorative rosette. Also referred to as *ribbons*.

roughing-off a term indicating that a horse or pony, having been stable-kept, is being turned out to grass. The roughing-off process means an adjustment of the feeding routine by omitting certain heat-giving food-stuffs, changing the exercise pattern and slowly reducing the use of rugs.

Royal Canadian Mounted Police, The the world-renowned 'Mounties', founded in 1873 as the North-West Mounted Police. The name was changed in 1920.

Royal International Horse Show a major horse show which takes place each July at which among the major show-jumping competitions are the King George Gold Cup and the Queen Elizabeth II Cup.

rugging-up the putting on of rugs.

rules for good feeding see under *feeding*.

running martingale a martingale which has one end attached to the girth and the other dividing into two straps each with a ring through which the reins pass before being affixed to the bit. (See illustration page 78.)

running out a horse or pony which deliberately avoids an obstacle by running away to one side is said to be 'running out'. This is penalised as for a disobedience and the obstacle must be retaken before moving on.

Russian Heavy Draught Horse a breed from the Ukraine region. The Russian Heavy Draught is used widely for agricultural purposes. Standing about 15 hands, it is strong and reliable and can work steadily for quite long periods.

S

saddle   a seat for a rider on the back of a horse. Special saddles are designed and made for many purposes. Some of these are listed below. See illustration overleaf.

saddle, all-purpose   see *saddle, general-purpose.*

saddle, dressage   a dressage saddle has a short and deeper seat than the general-purpose saddle. The flaps are straighter and the panel gives a little knee and thigh support.

saddle, general-purpose   designed with a forward panel and wide flaps. In general use and suitable for a variety of equestrian activities.

saddle, hunting   when specially made, the hunting saddle has no knee rolls and is shaped without the forward flaps of the general-purpose saddle.

saddle, jumping   a deep-seated saddle, cut forward and having knee rolls set into the panels.

saddle, racing   a small, lightweight saddle with flaps cut well forward.

saddle, showing   a saddle designed with straight flaps to show to advantage a horse or pony's shoulders and front.

saddle, side-   a saddle designed with two pommels, one placed diagonally above the other. The rider sits with both feet on the same side – not astride the horse. When seated side-saddle the rider will have the right leg over and around the higher pommel, and the left leg resting under and against the lower pommel. The left foot rests in the stirrup.

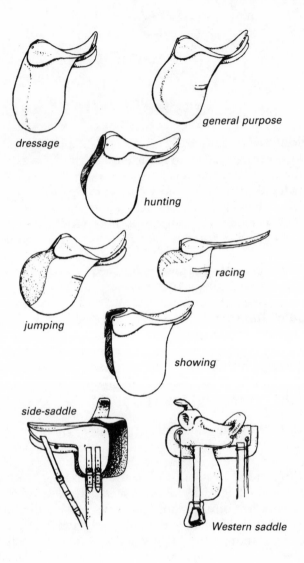

dressage

general purpose

hunting

jumping

racing

showing

side-saddle

Western saddle

Saddles

saddle, Western an American saddle having a deep seat and high cantle and pommel. Comfortable for those who ride for several hours at a time, the Western saddle is ornamental with most intricate designs on the leather-work.

saddle-bracket a metal or plastic bracket, fitted to the wall of a tack room, to hold saddles when not in use.

saddle-horse a trestle on which saddles are placed for storage or cleaning.

saddle, parts of the seven parts of a saddle (see illustration overleaf) are: **1** *tree*, the framework upon which a saddle is built; **2** the *panel*, the part which rests against the horse's back; **3** the *pommel*, the top front part; **4** the *cantle*, the back part; **5** the *seat*; **6** the *skirt*, the flap covering the stirrup bars; **7** the *saddle flaps*, against which the rider's legs rest.

saddle soap a specially prepared soap used with a dampened sponge to clean and help preserve the leather of saddles and other items of tack made from leather.

saddle tree the frame around which a saddle is built. Two types of tree are found – the rigid tree and the spring tree, both of which can be made from wood, fibreglass, metal or plastic.

saddler a craftsman who makes and repairs saddles and leather equipment used in riding.

saddlery see *tack*.

salt lick a block of salt fitted to a stable wall, or to a post near to where a grass-kept animal is fed.

sand crack a split which may occur in the wall of the hoof, running downwards from the coronet. A sand crack must not be left untreated, since this may cause acute lameness.

sawdust a bedding material which some owners find much easier to handle than other forms. Some horses and ponies find the dust and fine powder from sawdust affects their breathing; if this happens the bedding should be replaced by wood chips.

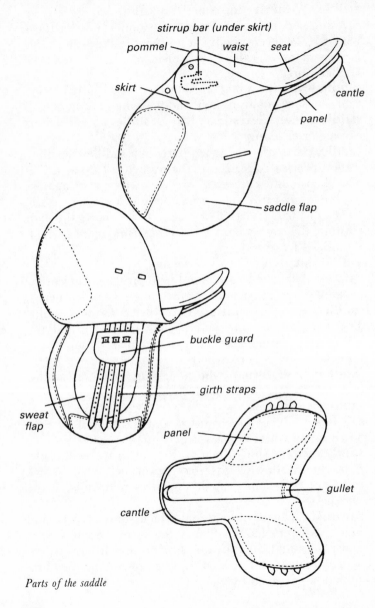

stirrup bar (under skirt)

pommel   waist   seat

skirt

cantle

panel

saddle flap

buckle guard

girth straps

sweat flap

panel

gullet

cantle

Parts of the saddle

schedule   a list giving details of classes and events and conditions of entry at a horse show.

Schockemöhle, Paul (West Germany)   a well-known rider who has represented his country many times in international competitions. In 1976 he won a silver medal with the German Team at the Montreal Olympics.

school   1 an area used for training and exercising; **2** to train a horse or pony.

schoolmaster   a horse or pony with wide experience and which has been well trained and schooled. This makes him ideally suited to younger and novice riders.

searcher   a tool used by a farrier.

seat   the position of a rider in the saddle.

seat of a saddle   the part of the saddle on which the rider sits.

service   the mating of a mare by a stallion.

sesamoids   the two small bones situated at the back of the fetlock which form part of that joint.

shank   the bone in a hind leg which extends from the knee to the fetlock. The corresponding bone in the foreleg is called a cannon bone.

shannon bone   the cannon bone of the hind leg; the shank (see above).

sheepskin noseband   a noseband frequently fitted on racehorses.

shelter   a shed or open-sided hut in a field into which horses and ponies can go in summer months to avoid heat and flies, and in winter to shelter from rain and severe weather. A shelter must always be positioned to ensure that the prevailing winds blow on the back of it and not into the open side.

Shetland   one of the nine British native pony breeds. Originating in the Shetland Islands, the breed is now known and loved throughout the world. Shetland ponies are extremely strong for their size and make good harness ponies. Measured in inches, not hands, the breed stands up to 40 in (100 cm); colours are mostly black, bay, brown, chestnut, grey, piebald and skewbald.

Shire a breed of heavy horse, considered by many to be the supreme example of that type. The Shire has a calm and gentle temperament, and its willingness to work is matched by the pleasure it appears to have when appearing at horse shows and agricultural shows. It is an excellent draught horse, with stamina, strength and obedience.

shoeing the making, fitting and fixing of shoes to horses and ponies.

shoulder-in a movement used in dressage.

Showing an all-embracing word for those competitions, in-hand or under saddle, at which a horse or pony or rider is judged according to conditions laid down in the schedule of classes at a show. Some showing classes are arranged to find the best rider, and in these cases the quality of the horse or pony being ridden should not be taken into account. In other showing classes the ability and scope of a horse or pony, in addition to conformation, condition and suitability, are the criteria by which a class is judged.

sickle hocks weak-looking hocks which appear shaped like a sickle.

side reins the leather straps which pass from a saddle to a bit and which are used in training and schooling.

silks the colours of an owner of a racehorse which are worn by a jockey.

simplex irons see *Australian Simplex Safety iron.*

sire the male parent of the foal.

Skelton, Nick (Great Britain) a most popular rider who won the Junior European Championship individual title in 1975. Has represented Great Britain on many occasions at most of the major show-jumping competitions in Europe and the United States. In December 1979 he broke the British record for the high jump.

skewbald a body colour with large irregular patches

of white and any colour other than black.

skip   a plastic container or wicker basket used in a stable when removing stained straw or other forms of bedding.

skirt   the part of a saddle which covers the stirrup bars.

Smith, Harvey (Great Britain)   a great personality and brilliant rider. Born in Yorkshire, he has over many years been a most successful show jumper at both national and international levels. A member of the Olympic Team in 1968 and 1972. His judgement and ability are recognised throughout the world.

Smith, Robert (Great Britain)   elder son of Harvey Smith and a great favourite throughout the British Isles. He has represented his country on several occasions.

snaffle bit   the older and most simple type of bit comprising either a single-jointed or straight mouthpiece. The single-jointed snaffle bit is made from metal and is illustrated on page 19. The unjointed or straight snaffle can be made of metal, vulcanite or rubber. The rings of the bit are circular or D-shaped, the latter reducing the risk of the lips being pinched.

snip   a white mark between the nostrils.

sock   a white fetlock.

sole   the under-portion of the hoof.

Somerville, Edith Oenone   a well-known author of many books featuring sport in Ireland. Born 1858: died 1949.

Spanish Riding School   the world-renowned riding establishment in Vienna at which the classical form of riding is taught and exhibited.

spavin, bog   a swelling on the inside of the hock.

spavin, bone   a bony growth on the back of the knee.

speak   the bark or bay of a hound on finding a scent of the fox. See *music*.

splint   a growth which forms between the cannon bone and the splint bone as a result of strain or jarring. Splints are more likely to occur in younger horses and ponies.

sporting phaeton a four-wheeled vehicle designed along the lines of a dog cart, with two seats back-to-back.

spotted horse see *Appaloosa*.

spread an obstacle such as an oxer, hog's back, parallel and water jump. Fences which have width, the opposite being the vertical or upright variety.

spring tree a saddle tree made to be more resilient than a rigid tree. It will enable the rider's seat and back aids to be more easily transmitted, and allows the seat of the saddle to 'give' to the movement of the horse's back.

spring wagon a type of vehicle or cart found in the United States.

spurs an artificial aid fitted to the heel of a rider.

stable the building in which horses and ponies are housed. The word stable can also mean an establishment or yard which has a number of horses and ponies. See *livery yard*.

stable bandages these should be the woollen variety. They are applied to avoid injury or adding to an existing injury. Stable bandages should never be fitted too tightly.

stable rubber a duster or cloth used in grooming.

stage coach a public coach which at one time carried passengers and luggage between towns and cities in Great Britain. The long journeys made by stage coaches were broken by stops at coaching inns found along the route. At these 'staging' posts the horses would either be rested or changed. Stage coaches first appeared in the early 1600s and ran to a very strict timetable.

stall a part of a stable in which a horse or pony is tied up. A stall, unlike a loose box, is without built-up walls and usually open-ended.

stallion a male horse, ungelded, aged four years or over.

standing back in show jumping, a horse is said to be

standing back when it takes off some distance in front of the obstacle.

standing martingale   one of the artificial aids, consisting of a leather strap with an adjustable loop which passes from the nose-band to the girth and is secured by a strap around the neck. (See illustration page 78.)

star   a head marking. A white diamond-shaped mark on a horse or pony's forehead. (See illustration page 60.)

stargazer   an expression used for a horse which carries its head too high.

steeplechase   a horse-race under Jockey Club Rules with a set number of obstacles including a water jump. The most famous of all steeplechases is the Grand National which takes place at Aintree, on the outskirts of Liverpool. In a steeplechase there are twelve obstacles in the first two miles and not more than six in each additional mile.

stifle   the joint in the hind leg which corresponds to the knee in a human.

stifle cap   the bone in front of the stifle joint.

stirrup bar   a bar found on the saddle and through which the stirrup leathers are fitted.

stirrup leathers   the adjustable straps to hold the stirrup irons. Fitted to a saddle by means of stirrup bars.

stirrups   shaped metal devices fitted to leathers which hang from a saddle and into which a rider's feet are placed.

stock   a shaped scarf made from linen or silk and tied round the rider's neck. Used in hunting and other equestrian activities, a stock is tied in a special way and fastened with a stock pin.

stocking   the name given to a white leg marking which extends as far as the knee or hock.

strangles   a contagious throat infection of horses.

Stanhope phaeton   a lightweight phaeton which has seats for four people facing forwards. The Stanhope phaeton has a full lock which enables it to be turned round in little space. Driven by a pair or single horse.

straw a bedding material.

strip down to remove the saddle from the horse or pony in a showing class to enable it to be judged for conformation.

stripe a narrow white line running down the face.

Stubbs, George an equestrian artist. Born 1724: died 1806.

stud **1** a place at which horses and ponies are bred; **2** a metal cap fitted to the shoes of horses to enable them to have a better grip when the 'going' demands it.

Suffolk Punch a breed of heavy horse originating in East Anglia. The Suffolk is the oldest of the breeds of heavy horse found in Great Britain. It is still used for work on farms, as well as for pulling brewers' drays in city streets. Clean-legged and always chesnut in colour (note the way this word is spelt when describing this breed), the Suffolk stands up to 17 hands.

sulky a low, two-wheeled vehicle used in trotting and pacing races.

summer sheet a sheet made from cotton or linen to take the place of a day rug during warmer summer months.

a summer sheet

surcingle a belt made from jute or hemp which can be used in place of a roller to secure a rug or saddle.

Surrey a four-wheeled vehicle used in the United States. A Surrey has two forward-facing seats. Many have a cloth top with fringes on the sides.

suspension the position of a horse or pony and rider when in mid-air over a jump.

sweat flaps made to keep sweat from the saddle flaps. Sweat flaps also prevent buckles from causing discomfort to the horse or pony.

sweet itch an irritable skin condition of the crest, withers or croup.

T

Tables a word which is sometimes found in schedules of classes and events. The Tables, which are applicable at all shows affiliated to the BSJA, or jumped according to the rules of the FEI, are used to determine the nature of the competition and any jump-off procedure.

tack or saddlery means the saddle, bridle, martingale and so on with which a horse is 'harnessed' for work.

tack room the place where saddlery and other items used for the horse are kept. No item of equipment should be left dirty. The stripping-down, cleaning and putting up of all pieces used is an essential part of stable routine.

tail the tail includes the dock and the hair on the tail.

tail bandage the bandage used to protect a tail against rubbing or injury when travelling and to make the hair lie neatly at the top of the tail. Tail bandages are usually made from crêpe or stockinette.

tail guard a leather or cloth-made protective device which is fitted over a tail bandage. (See page 115.)

take-off the point at which a horse or pony lifts its forehand and springs up from the hocks when jumping.

taking off 1 an expression used in jumping; 2 in driving to describe the taking of horses or ponies from a vehicle. In this context 'taking off' is the reverse of 'putting to'.

taking off too late said of a horse or pony when it gets too near to an obstacle to be jumped.

taking off too soon said of a horse or pony which stands back from the correct point of take-off.

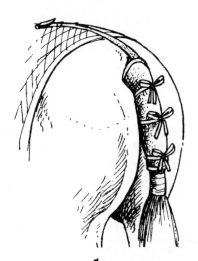

Tail guard

take-off side   the approach side of the obstacle.

tandem   being driven in tandem describes a team of two horses positioned one behind the other.

tandem cart   a two-wheeled vehicle with a high box seat pulled by a tandem team.

tandem team   the team of horses used in a tandem (see above).

teeth   male horses have forty teeth when the jaws are fully developed, mares thirty-six. Of these, twelve are incisors (six in each jaw), four canine or tushes (these are found in the male only, one on each side both in the upper and lower jaw), and twenty-four molars (twelve in each jaw).

temperature   the normal temperature for a horse is 38°C (100.5°F).

tendon boots   specially designed boots to support and protect the tendons.

tendons   the bands of tough fibrous tissue which connect muscles with bones.

tendons, strained   a lameness in a horse or pony caused when the tendon fibres are torn or injured.

Tennessee Walking Horse a breed, found mostly in the United States of America, recognised by its kindly nature, its ability under saddle and expansive gait. Usually standing between 15.2 and 16 hands, it has no restriction as to colour.

tetanus a dangerous disease which can enter the body by an infected wound. Foals and young horses are particularly susceptible and prevention is possible by giving anti-tetanus serum injections.

Thoroughbred with the Arab, the Thoroughbred is recognised as a 'universal horse' and one that plays a considerable part in horse breeding throughout the world. Primarily used for horse-racing, the Thoroughbred is also used as a cross to produce all types of saddle horses. Predominant colours are bay, grey, brown, chestnut and black (see *Arab*). The ancestry of the English Thoroughbred can be traced back to the Byerley Turk, Darley Arabian and Godolphin Arabian (see also the entries under these names).

three-day event a combined training competition, now coming under the heading of Horse Trials held over three consecutive days, this is considered the supreme test of the ability, precision and courage of a horse and rider. Day one is given over to dressage; day two to the speed and endurance test of the steeplechase and cross-country course; and day three to show jumping.

three-quarter-bred a term used to describe a cross between a Thoroughbred and a half-bred mare.

throat lash a narrow leather strap, sometimes called a throat latch, which is part of a bridle and which is buckled under the throat to prevent the bridle from slipping over the horse's ears. To check that a throat lash is not too tightly buckled three fingers should be able to be placed between the strap and the horse's throat.

thrush an inflammation of the frog. Thrush produces a noticeable discharge and a bad smell. Among the causes of thrush are: neglect of the feet of horses and ponies; bad shoeing; poor stable drainage, giving rise to permanently wet feet.

time allowed   the time set by which a competitor must complete a jumping competition if he or she is not to incur time faults. The time allowed is worked out by measuring the track a horse or pony would take, without attempting to take corners too sharply, in going from the start to the finish, and assessing the appropriate speed at which the competition would be ridden. The distance of the track is then divided by the speed set for the competition; for example, a show-jumping track of 450 metres (492 yards), ridden at a speed of 300 metres (378 yards) per minute, would give a time allowed of one and a half minutes.

time limit   the time found by doubling the time allowed. Exceeding the time limit, for whatever reason, means elimination from that particular competition.

toeing knife   a part of a farrier's tool kit.

tooth rasp   a rasp used by a veterinary surgeon for filing-down and smoothing rough edges of teeth. See *rasp*.

trace clip   a clip which removes the hair from the belly and top of the legs. Illustrated on page 33.

Traekehner   a horse of great quality and bred with many Thoroughbred characteristics. Its origin was at the world-renowned Traekehner Stud, founded in East Prussia (now Poland) in 1732. Standing between 16 and 16.3 hands the breed is made-up of all solid colours. The Traekehner has great stamina, and is widely used as a riding horse.

tracheotomy   an operation carried out to ease breathing problems.

track   in jumping, the 'track' is the path measured to establish time. (See *time allowed*.) It is also the path undertaken by a competitor between start and finish.

traffic-proof   a horse or pony is said to be traffic-proof

117

when it can be ridden quietly and safely in traffic.

trandem   three horses harnessed to two poles and driven abreast.

trap   a term in general use for any small horsedrawn vehicle or cart.

travers   a movement in dressage in two tracks in which the horse moves as in a half-pass, with its hindlegs on the inner track and the forelegs on the inner track. Known also as a 'head to the wall' movement.

treble   a combination obstacle found in show jumping in which three separate elements must be jumped, and though each counts separately as far as faults are concerned, the three together count as one obstacle. See *combination*.

tree   see *saddle tree*.

trekking   a word used to describe riding in organised groups across open countryside.

trimming   the tidying of the hair of a head, mane, tail or 'feathers'.

triple bar   an obstacle built to a staircase design.

troika a method, mostly used in Russia, of harnessing three horses side by side, or with one in front and a pair behind.

trot one of the four natural paces (gaits). The trot is a two-time pace, and when trotting the sequence is near fore and off hind together (known as the left diagonal) and off fore and near hind together (the right diagonal).

trot, collected a slow trot, with the horse moving well up to the bit with good impulsion.

trot, extended a pace in which the stride is lengthened by correct application of the leg aids. The rhythm of the trot at the lengthened stride must be maintained, and the horse's neck allowed to extend without the rider losing contact through the bit.

trot, rising the action of the rider when rising from the saddle at one beat of the trot sequence, missing the next, and returning to the saddle on the next.

trot, sitting the action of a rider when remaining in the saddle and not 'rising' at the trot.

turned out describing a horse or pony put out to grass.

turnout an expression used to describe the general appearance, cleanliness and presentation of a horse or pony, its saddlery and rider.

type a type of horse is not a breed. Included among the 'types' found in Great Britain are the hunter, cob, hack, polo pony, etc.

Tyteca, Ferdi (Belgium) a well-travelled and skilful rider who has represented Belgium many times in international competitions.

U

underface a horse or pony asked to jump an obstacle too low for his capability is said to be 'underfaced'. The opposite of underfacing is overfacing.

united a horse or pony is considered to be cantering true or 'united' when it leads with the near fore and near hind or vice versa.

Cantering 'united'

unsound a term used to describe a lame animal.

upright any obstacle or fence built on a vertical plane. This type of fence might consist of poles, planks or a gate. A wall is also considered to be an upright obstacle. No penalties or faults are awarded for any part other than the top element which falls in the act of jumping.

V

velvet cap the hard hat essential for all who ride. Young riders are advised to wear a riding hat at all times when in the stable yard or paddock.

vertical see *upright*.

veterinary surgeon a highly trained and skilled person who practises veterinary medicine and/or surgery by diagnosing and treating illness and disease in animals.

vices the common vices of a horse or pony are kicking, biting, bucking, rearing, napping, resisting, crib-biting and weaving. (Apart from kicking and biting, which are self-explanatory, see separate entries under these headings.)

vixen a female fox.

W

wagon a term used in the United States to describe a four-wheeled vehicle.

waist of a saddle the narrowest part of the seat.

Waler a breed of saddle horse from New South Wales, Australia. Used for most equestrian activities, the Waler is perhaps best known for its work on cattle stations.

walk the first of the natural paces (gaits), made up in four-time. At a walk the sequence is near hind, near fore, off hind, off fore.

walk, collected a short and controlled pace carried out with good impulsion and light hands. A horse or pony at a collected walk should move forward with a raised and arched neck, its hind feet touching the ground immediately behind the footprints of the forefeet.

walk, extended an open and extended stride, but one not to be hurried. An extended walk is carried out on a loose rein and the rider must ensure he is in contact at all times.

walk, ordinary one of the four natural paces (gaits). The walk is a steady pace in which the four legs of the horse follow each other in four-time, each step being positive and clear. When the walk is slovenly and not in a regular rhythm it is said to be 'broken' or 'disunited'.

wall an obstacle in show jumping, the bricks of which must be capable of being knocked down. Fixed walls, made from brick, concrete, stone or wood, are found in cross-country courses and at horse trials.

wall eye an eye with a pinkish-white or bluish-white

appearance due to a lack of pigment in the iris.

wall of the hoof the wall is made up in three parts: the heel, quarters or sides, and toe. It is that part of the hoof seen when a foot has been placed firmly on the ground.

warble fly the warble fly lays its eggs on the lowest part of the legs of a horse. When the eggs hatch the larvae move round the body, finally reaching the back, where they appear as small, hard lumps under the skin. Treatment consists of removing the larvae from each lump.

water an essential for both stable-kept and grass-kept horses and ponies. Those kept at grass ideally should have piped water to a trough to ensure a continuous fresh supply. When containers are used in a paddock they must frequently be emptied, cleaned and refilled. All horses must have fresh water available at all times.

water brush a brush which is dampened and used on the mane and tail.

water jump an obstacle found in show jumping.

weaving a nervous habit and vice by which a horse or pony weaves its head from side to side when in the stable. Weaving is a dangerous habit as other horses tend to copy it. Although it is not likely to be completely stopped, an anti-weaving device, fitted to a lower stable door, can minimise the problem.

Welsh cob see below.

Welsh ponies the Welsh ponies comprise one of the nine British native pony breeds. There are four sections of Welsh pony. Section A, the Welsh Mountain pony; Section B, the Welsh pony; Section C, the Welsh cob; Section D, the Welsh cob, but larger than Section C. Sections refer to sections as in the Welsh Pony and Cob Society Stud Book).

Welsh pony, Section A: the Welsh Mountain pony the smallest of the four sections, the Welsh Mountain pony stands up to 12 hands, and is one of the most beautiful and intelligent of all pony breeds. All colours are accepted in the Breed Register other than piebald and skewbald.

Welsh pony, Section B a pony standing a little more than those in Section A – between 12 and 13.2 hands. An ideal pony for children, being sure-footed and friendly in nature.

Welsh cob, Section C a strong, hardy and active pony, usually between 13 and 14 hands. Bigger in build than either the Section A or B, this sturdier animal is nearer to the cob in both appearance and temperament.

Welsh cob, Section D a kindly, willing, active and obedient pony, perhaps the best all-round pony of all. The cob stands between 14 and 15 hands and, as with all sections of the Welsh can be any colour other than piebald or skewbald.

Weymouth or double bridle this is made up from a bridoon and a curb or Weymouth bit with a fixed or movable mouthpiece and a curb chain with a lipstrap. As it has two bits, the double bridle or Weymouth can be most severe if not understood, and it is not advised for use by the young and inexperienced. See illustration on page 24.

wheelers in driving, the horses nearest to the vehicle. See *leaders*.

Whitaker, John a skilful rider with extremely sound judgement. Has represented Great Britain on many occasions. In 1982 helped Britain gain a team bronze medal in the World Championships in Dublin, and was third in the World Cup.

white face a face which has a white forehead, nose and muzzle.

white coronet, fetlock, heels, pastern the colour on that particular part of a horse or pony's leg.

white flag a flag used to denote the extreme left-hand side of an obstacle (see *red flag*).

Whyte-Melville. George John a poet and author who

124

specialised in equestrian subjects. Born 1821: died 1878.

Wiltfang, Gerd (Germany)   the 1980 World and European Champion. A popular and brilliant rider who has competed throughout the world. He won a gold medal with the German team in the 1972 Olympic Games at Munich.

windgall   a painless swelling of the area above and behind the fetlock joint.

windsucking   a horse is a 'windsucker' when it sucks in air and makes a gulping noise when swallowing. Such an animal is classed unsound.

winter out   a horse or pony left out in a field or paddock during winter months.

wisp   a pad made by twisting straw into a type of ball. Used after grooming to tone up the horse's muscles and promote circulation.

withers   the highest part of a horse's back at the base of the crest line of the neck.

worming   all horses and ponies require regular treatment to rid them of worms. This should be carried out on the instructions of a veterinary surgeon.

wrangler   a word used in the United States to indicate a cowhand or cowboy. To 'wrangle' means to round-up or collect.

Y

yard a word used to mean a stable yard and also to mean the business or premises at which particular equestrian activities are carried out, e.g. a livery yard.

yearling a colt or filly having reached its first but not second anniversary of birth.

yellow dun see *dun*.

Yorkshire boot a protective boot or covering for a fetlock. Fitted to prevent injury to a horse or pony liable to brushing.

Z

zebra marks the stripes found on the limbs, neck, withers and quarters of some horses and ponies.

Zetland phaeton a vehicle similar to a four-wheeled dog cart. The two seats are placed back to back and are set much higher than in most other carts and phaetons.

zig-zag an obstacle constructed from timber posts and rails placed at angles to each other, used in a cross-country course. The horse can either jump over the point of the V or over the angled sides.